FERRETS
CARE AND BREEDING

FERRETS
CARE AND BREEDING

Ian C. Rickard

The Crowood Press

First published in 2005 by
The Crowood Press Ltd
Ramsbury, Marlborough
Wiltshire SN8 2HR

www.crowood.com

British Library Cataloguing-in-Publication Data
A catalogue record for this book is available from the British
Library.

ISBN 1 86126 796 7

Typeset by NBS Publications, Basingstoke, UK

Printed and bound in Great Britain by The Cromwell Press,
Trowbridge

Contents

— 1 —

Classification

Our friend the ferret has a long history. Before we can consider that, however, I feel that it is prudent to look back on their origins and scientific classification, and the best place to start is at the beginning with their classification.

All life as we know it that has been discovered is classified in scientific lists and the scientific name given is known as a binomial. That is to say, a creature is given a name, its species group is identified, which is grouped further still into a family of like creatures, then set into an order. Finally, this order is made part of a greater assemblage called a class.

CLASS

So, let us begin this journey, from the class forward; the ferret is of the class Mammalia. It is a mammal, and one of in excess of 4,000 species that share this class. Put simply, mammals are creatures that have a spine, have hair to insulate their body (although not all are completely covered – take us humans for example), nurture their progeny or young with milk that is delivered via mammary glands, and the articulation of their jaw is unique. Another attribute among animals with backbones that is again unique to mammals is that many are able to communicate through complicated systems of scents and odours.

These scents and odours, whether fair or foul, are produced and secreted through scent glands and musk glands situated at various points of the anatomy, dependent on the specific species. They can also be emitted through the skin in carriers such as perspiration.

The odours produced can, and do, serve to communicate many things to other creatures, not necessarily only within their own species group. The messages contained within these sensory 'parcels' may be designed to attract or repel other creatures, and can range from signifying the limit to territorial boundaries, gender assignation and reproductive status, and also in the case of some species, including ferrets, warnings and fear.

Beyond these few similarities there is a startling array of dissimilarities in the way that individual species have evolved, both physically and behaviourally.

ORDER

The next level of classification is the order. The ferret is of the order Carnivora, which is the order of mammalian flesh-eating creatures or carnivores. It also includes cats, dogs, bears, and so on, along with many others. There are actually seven families, consisting of ninety-three genera and over 230 species in this order.

FAMILY

We now progress to the next level of classification, which is the family – ferrets are of the family Mustelidae. Mustelids, which include badgers and otters, are possibly the most successful family of the Carnivora, and its oldest. They are also the largest family of the Carnivora, numbering nearly seventy species, in more than twenty-five genera. This is nearly twice as many as the next largest family, Herpestidae.

Mustelids are native to all continents except Australia and Antarctica, although they have been introduced to New Zealand. Consequently, mustelids survive in all climates, whether arctic or tropical; they live on land, in rivers and the open sea, and also in trees.

Skulls of mustelids generally have a tendency to be long, elongated from front to back, flattened in profile view (seen from the side), and 'triangular' in plan view (seen from the top), tapering towards the tip or snout.

Notable features of this family are their reproductive habits. The sexes live separately for most of the year, and hostility usually ensues should they meet. The exception to this status is during the mating season, when there is a temporary 'truce'. Copulation is both prolonged and very intense or rough. It is necessarily so to induce the female to ovulate.

The duration of this prolonged mating can have serious safety implications whilst the mating pair is actually involved in the act of coitus. The risk of attacks from predators is greatly increased during

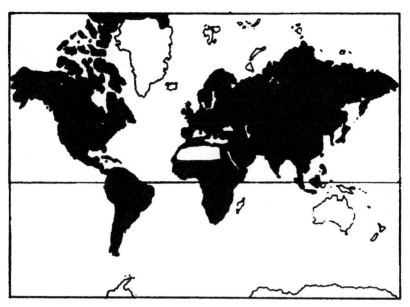

Distribution of the family Mustelidae.

the coupling, and the mating pair is significantly disadvantaged with regard to self protection during this time. These safety concerns, however, are outweighed when balanced on the scales of procreation by the fact that with ovulation being induced during copulation, failure to conceive is most unlikely, and reproduction is virtually guaranteed.

In most mammals the fertilized egg, once having developed into a blastocyst, or ball of cells, implants itself into the wall of the uterus where it continues its foetal development. However, in some of the species in this family delayed implantation is possible. Delayed implantation is where the blastocyst floats freely, completely unattached and with development suspended within the uterus until the required circumstances demanded by nature are in place. Delays in implantation can be for as little as a few days, or for as long as ten months in some species. The implantation will only occur when certain criteria are met; these criteria may and do vary from species to species. Ferrets, however, do not have delayed implantation, and development of the embryo ensues as soon as the blastocyst implants itself in the uterus wall post-coitus.

SUBFAMILY

From here we progress to the subfamily, which in this case is Mustelinae. Within this group there are ten genera and over thirty species, which include weasels, mink, polecats and martens to name but a few, as well as our friend the ferret. When considered as a group of carnivores, Mustelinae are one of the widest spread groups in the world.

All of the species in this group are terrestrial hunters, mainly sourcing their prey from the rodent species and birds. Their teeth are consequently evolved and ideally suited to killing and cutting up their meals. Feeding is not usually indiscriminate, as they tend to live in and around areas where their ideal prey exists.

All species tend to eat creatures suited to their own size; the smaller the predator, the smaller its prey, and therefore the larger the predator the larger the prey species as they can gain a greater return for their expended effort in taking said prey. Having said this, they will obviously eat from each other's 'menus' if their ideally suited prey is not available for whatever reason, assuming that they are capable of making the kill.

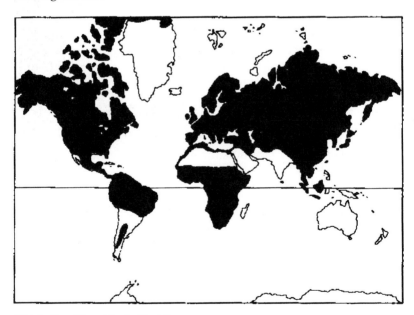

Distribution of the subfamily Mustelinae.

An interesting trait of weasels and polecats, and of course ferrets, is that they will often sit up on their haunches or hind legs to get a better view of their surroundings than would be obtainable if they remained on all fours. Whilst this will undoubtedly increase their field of view, it is probably of most use defensively by permitting them to see the approach of larger creatures that may pose a threat to their safety, as their eyesight over anything but short distances is poor, and only really detects movement.

SPECIES

After the subfamily comes the species. Carolus Linnaeus first described the ferret for classification in 1758 in 'Mammalia Ferae' which was first published in *Systema Naturae: Regnum Animale*. Linnaeus was a naturalist and a physician of Swedish descent and he developed the binomial method of classification that is still used today. On page 46 of 'Mammalia Ferae', entry number six is the

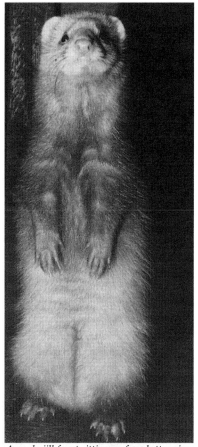

A sandy jill ferret sitting up for a better view.

European polecat, whose species is listed as *Mustela putorius*. Entry number seven is the ferret, which is listed as *Mustela furo*.

Much later, in the late 1970s and early 1980s, when chromosomal evidence became available, it was decided purely by chromosomal count that both the European polecat and the ferret were in fact not separate species as previously thought, but were indeed the same species as they both had forty chromosomes.

SUBSPECIES

Because of the rules of priority, and the fact that the polecat was named first, it kept the species name *Mustela putorius*. The ferret, because it was considered to be a domesticated version of the polecat, now became considered as a subspecies of the polecat and was given the subspecies name *furo*. Hence the ferret now became *Mustela putorius furo*.

This, in my opinion, is rather a derogatory term, as *furo* is derived from *furonem*, the Latin for thief. The origin of its use may be due to the mask on the faces of polecat-coloured ferrets being similar to the masks used by highwaymen and robbers in times past, or, more likely, it may be derived from ferrets being renowned stealers of eggs, and indeed killers of chickens. This observation would have been particularly noticed by man when the thefts were from domesticated chicken housing.

The consideration of this latter possibility can be taken further when you take into account the French translation of the name polecat, which is *poulechat*. When this name is directly translated into English it becomes 'chickencat'. The earliest mention of the term *furo* and its linking to and association with ferret-like creatures was actually by Isidore of Seville in AD600, as will be explained later.

Therefore, at the end of this classification trail we have the ferrets' official scientific designation. It is: *Mustela putorius furo*, or *M. p. furo* to abbreviate it correctly.

EUROPEAN OR STEPPE?

There are, however, contradictions regarding the ancestry of the ferret, with some schools of thought claiming, as noted above, that it is descended from the European polecat, whereas there are others who believe it to be descended from the Steppe polecat.

In an attempt to throw some light on this subject we can take into account the chromosomal evidence, although it is far from conclusive. Whilst being correct as far as it goes, it is only concerned with the karyotype, that is the number of, and the external morphology of, the chromosomes. It does not take into account the genome, which is the total amount of genetic information that an organism possesses.

Based solely on the karyotypic chromosomal evidence the ferret is most likely to be more closely related to the European polecat than the Steppe polecat. (The Steppe polecat's scientific designation is

Mustela eversmanni, being so named after the German zoologist, Professor Dr E. Eversmann, who lived between 1794 and 1860, and is credited with its discovery.) Because the ferret has forty chromosomes as does the European polecat (whilst the Steppe polecat has only thirty-eight), it is considered to be a descendant thereof. Either way, because the chromosomal evidence and studies to date have only been concerned with the karyotype, and to the best of my knowledge have not been extended to the genome, they can only be considered to be, in effect, circumstantial evidence, and therefore not wholly conclusive.

There have been other studies, specifically on the cranium and the teeth, which contradict the aforementioned viewpoint. These studies actually raise a claim that the ferret is related more closely to the Steppe polecat than to the European polecat. If this is the case, and it is not beyond the realms of possibility, there would have had to have been a stage in the evolution of the species whereby some genetic event caused an increase in the number of chromosomes.

Whichever of the possibilities that you choose to consider as being the ancestor of our current friend the ferret, I am sure you will always be able to find someone to contradict you somewhere.

A further possibility, and one that will muddy the waters further, but has to be considered, is that the ferret as we know it today may actually be descended from another creature that is now extinct! I do wonder on occasions if we will ever know for certain.

2

History

Mustelids, as previously stated, are a very old family of animals. Ferrets, in particular, appear to have first been mentioned, historically speaking, around 450BC in 'The Acharnians', a comedy by Aristophanes, although some believe that they were kept as pets by the Egyptians before cats gained their favour. Ferrets were again mentioned later by Aristotle (384BC–322BC) in his *Historia Animalium*, this mention being dated *circa* 350BC.

If we take these earliest apparent reports at face value then it can be concluded that there are records of ferrets, or at least domesticated polecats, being used by mankind to hunt rodents for food dating back in the region of two and a half millennia.

However, the first generally accepted reference was not until 63BC. This reference was made by Strabo in his *Geographica*, and was an account of a Libyan animal that was bred, in captivity, specifically for the purpose of being entered to rabbit warrens in order to bolt or otherwise remove the occupants physically with the assistance of a human counterpart.

The creature in this account was said to have always been muzzled when worked. It was described as having either bolted the rabbits (bolting is the term applied when the ferret pursues the rabbit until it exits the warren in which it was living), or alternatively to have gripped them with its claws and then been pulled out, complete with its prey, on the end of a lead or line controlled by the person who had entered the ferret or been left with it in his charge. These reports of a ferret being worked are given credence by the fact that a Moroccan tribe, the Ruafa, are believed still to work them in this manner today.

A further support to this report was the fact that when Linnaeus classified the species that he named *Mustela putorius*, he geographically situated it in Africa. Complications arise here, though, because, as stated previously, whilst the majority of scientists involved believe that the ferret is a descendant of either *Mustela putorius* or *Mustela eversmanni* (European Polecat or Steppe Polecat, respectively), neither of these species actually originates from Africa!

These earliest accounts, as with many things from that time in history, are steeped in controversy. This is due to the fact that different experts and scholars tend to contradict each other as to the exact translation of the original Greek accounts.

Pliny's *Natural History*, dating from AD23, gives mention to both the rabbit and the ferret. The ferret does not appear to have specific mention in the Bible, although some early translations of this text, namely the older King James versions, translated one particular word from Leviticus as 'ferret'. These references are in Leviticus, Chapter XI, 29–30. Here the ferret was listed as *trayf*, and it was an animal that the Jews were forbidden to eat. However, these earliest translations have come to be extremely controversial as *trayf*, apparently, could mean any small mustelid. Newer translations of this text reject this as being a translation of ferret, claiming it as an error, and their interpretation is either 'gecko' or 'lizard'.

By AD600 the ferret was firmly cast in its role in the hunting of rabbits. This was written of by Isidore, the Bishop of Seville, who was born in Cartagena, Spain, and lived between AD560 and 4 April 636. He wrote in his book *Patrologie* of an animal used in the hunting of rabbits. Isidore called this creature *furo*, derived from *furonem*, the Latin for thief. This is quite probably, although by no means definitely, where the subspecies part of the binomial designation of *furo* for ferret originates. Somewhat later, in 1221, Genghis Khan is also reputed to have used ferrets on hunting forays in Afghanistan.

The rabbit, without whom we may not have domesticated the ferret, was to begin as an indigenous species of Spain and North Africa, although it had previously been seen feeding on the eastern shores of Spain by the Phoenicians *circa* 1100BC.

Basically, until the advent of the Roman period in history the rabbit had not spread beyond the Iberian peninsula, northern Africa and the south of France. The Romans captured rabbits, and sought to keep them in compounds or areas called 'warrens' that were convenient for them to 'harvest' from at will for the table. Needless to say, with the rabbits' consummate burrowing skills, it did not take long for them to escape these artificial confines and set up colonies of their own, outside the boundaries set down by their previous captors. The reproductive rate of rabbits meant that they soon covered large areas of the lands to which they were brought, wreaking havoc as they went.

Rabbits were also helped by monks to expand their realms of occupancy. Monks are in fact credited with probably being the first selective breeders of rabbits. They decided that the unborn foetuses and newly born kittens of rabbits would be classified as 'not meat', and as such they were able to eat them during periods of fasting. Therefore they kept rabbits in warrens, as did the Romans, and bred them in order to eat at these times. Not surprisingly, as in the case of the Romans, it did not take the captive rabbits long to devise means of escape and develop colonies of their own in the wild.

Humans also intervened even more blatantly in the spread of the rabbit. Whereas the Romans and the monks originally kept captive rabbits in warrens from which they subsequently accidentally escaped to set up their own wild colonies, sailors actually carried rabbits aboard ships to leave behind on various islands in order that they would breed and so create a self-propagating food source for the future. Ships stopping off at these islands could then take some of the rabbits as a fresh food source.

Sadly, this uninformed and cavalier practice caused some indigenous island species to be wiped out, as they were not equipped to compete with the actions and habits of the newcomer to their habitats. As a result of this rapid spread of rabbits, and the devastation that went with them, the ferrets' future as an ally of man in an attempt to control them was firmly secured.

It is unclear when the rabbit was actually introduced to British shores, but it is likely that the ferret was brought along at the same time. Many claim that the rabbit was brought over by the Romans to be reared as a fresh food source for the military, as noted above. However, there are other authorities who believe that the introduction of rabbits to Britain was carried out by the invading Normans, who kept them as a fresh food source in a similar manner to that of the Romans.

However and wherever rabbits were taken by man, it is reasonably safe to assume that at the same time he also took the ferret, because the ferret is by far the most efficient method of removing the rabbit from his subterranean dwelling when required for food.

Pursuant to the Norman Conquest, ferrets are clearly recorded as being in Great Britain. These records are both in the form of written records and also pictorial works. As a point of interest, the first-recorded rabbit colony in Britain was that on the Scilly Isles in 1176.

By the time of the dawn of the Middle Ages in Britain the ferret was widely used for the hunting of rabbits. Somewhat later, there is incontrovertible evidence of ferrets being used against rabbits in Britain. This is recorded on a court roll dating from 1223, and there are records of the Royal Court actually having a ferreter in 1281.

A picture dating from approximately 1325 that comes from Queen Mary's Psalter depicts two well-dressed women entering a ferret to a netted rabbit bury. Although it is a very simplistic work, there is no doubt as to its contents. The Psalter was actually presented to the Queen more than two centuries after the picture's production. Gaston, Comte de Foix, in 1387 in his *Livre de Chasse*, showed drawings of ferreting in progress with purse nets and a muzzled ferret.

Unfortunately, the practice of muzzling ferrets in order that they are prevented from killing their prey underground is still adhered to by some today. If the ferret is restrained in this manner, and comes upon a rival such as a rat in the course of its work, it will be unable to defend itself and is quite likely to be severely injured, or possibly even killed. Also, if the ferret should be lost, it will be unable to support itself and will starve to death. In the defence of some of those who muzzle their ferrets, however, some only use very thin cotton that will rot quickly in order that, should the ferret be lost, it will soon be able to feed itself. This is, of course, of no benefit to the ferret should it need to defend itself against a predator or other creature.

Having said this, muzzling is probably the least harmful form of oral restraint that has been employed by ferreters over the years. Other means of restraint that have been employed in the past, and may still be today by some inhumane keepers, are nothing short of cruel and abusive. One such other form of restraint is 'coping'. This is the breaking off of the ferret's canine teeth with instruments such as pliers. The implementation of this foul deed, generally speaking, is often attributed to gypsies and the like. Another equally abhorrent practice is that of stitching the ferret's lips together in order that it cannot open its mouth far enough to deliver bites to its prey.

To return to Britain in the Middle Ages, there are many references to ferrets being owned by high-ranking officials of the Church. These records serve to illustrate just how important rabbits, and thus ferrets, were to the Church and its establishments of the time. In addition to the Church, rabbits were also kept by lords of the various manors throughout the land, the nobility, and other landed gentry. These people set aside special fields for the occupancy of their rabbits, and within them built warrens for them to live in. This was obviously done in an attempt to keep them contained and stop them wandering to pastures new; however, as with the Romans and monks in previous times, some of the rabbits soon absconded to expand their realms of occupation.

However, with these areas created, they needed to be maintained and the rabbits taken care of. This task was probably more industrious than the landowners wished to indulge in themselves, so they were put in a position of needing to employ staff to carry out the day-to-day duties associated with the husbandry of their rabbits. With the area where the rabbits were kept being called a 'warren', it was therefore a logical progression that the person charged with its maintenance was called a 'warrener'.

These warreners were of great importance to their employers. They were usually quite well paid, and provided with a house to live in. In addition to this, they were usually provided with at the very least a room in which to keep the ferrets in their cages or barrels. Some landowners even built buildings specifically for housing the ferrets.

It was the duty of these warreners to take care of the upkeep of the warren and the rabbits, and to trap and kill any other predators that might decide that this was a convenient place to obtain a meal. In so doing, they ensured that there were plenty of rabbits for the table as and when required by their employer. As with many other surname-to-job relationships (blacksmith – Smith, for example), this is the derivation of present-day surnames such as Warren, Warrener and so on.

Rabbits had become a very important part of the food chain, and therefore ferreting also became correspondingly popular. Many people kept ferrets, and consequently the poaching of rabbits from landowners' property became a significant problem. In an attempt to curtail this activity and to protect the landowners' food sources and incomes, a law was passed in 1390 restricting the ownership of ferrets to those whose annual salary exceeded forty shillings. This being a very high salary at the time, it precluded any but the wealthy from ferret ownership. The fact that this law was created and passed serves to illustrate just how important rabbits, and by association ferrets, were to local economies.

A note to be mentioned here, simply because it is chronologically apt, is the origin of the collective noun employed for a group of ferrets, this being a 'business'. There have been other terms coined by some, but the correct term is business. The earliest known reference to a group of ferrets having its own collective name is made in a book called 'The Boke of St Albans', written by Dame Juliana Berners, and printed in 1468. In this book a list can be found of 'the companys of beestys and fowleys'. Within this list the collective term for ferrets is given as a 'besynes of ferrettis'. It does not take much of a stretch of the imagination to see how this has been modified over time to become the 'business of ferrets' as we know it today.

At this point in history when ferrets were being worked they needed to be recovered by the ferreters, or else dug out. If digging was

The fifteenth-century Franco-Burgundian tapestry. Courtesy of Glasgow City Council (Museums)

required, a liner (usually a large hob ferret with a line or cord attached to his collar) was entered to the bury to determine the location of the errant ferret, which would often be with a rabbit that it had killed. Once static, the line could be dug along to the location of the ferret. The alternative was, if possible, to call the ferrets out. The practice of calling ferrets out, often with the use of a flute, has been said by some to be what the story of 'The Pied Piper of Hamelin' was actually based on.

The art of ferreting is illustrated, somewhat crowdedly I might add, in a fifteenth-century Franco-Burgundian tapestry that is now in the Burrell Collection in Glasgow. This work shows peasants ferreting for rabbits. It is a very busy work with people, dogs and ferrets all eagerly up for the chase. Some artistic licence has to be allowed for in the depiction of what I assume are supposed to be purse nets of some description, as I cannot believe that if the work is accurate they would actually close. If, on the other hand, they are supposed to be some form of 'drop net', then I would be inclined to believe that, considering the speed of the rabbits fleeing their ferret pursuers, far more would escape than be caught, making the exercise incredibly inefficient.

Also in the fifteenth century, another artistic work in the form of a portrait was painted by Leonardo da Vinci in Italy. It is actually entitled 'Lady with an Ermine', but is also called 'Lady with the Ferret' by some. It is a picture of a woman holding a white ferret in her arms.

Moving onward in time, there is another artistic work called the 'Ermine Portrait' of Queen Elizabeth I which hangs in Hatfield House. This sixteenth-century work by Nicholas Hilliard (1547–1619) shows the Queen, heavily bejewelled and richly dressed, with a small ermine or stoat on her left sleeve that bears a coronet around its neck.

It is in fact unlikely that a stoat could be as tame and well handled as this one is portrayed to be, and it is this consideration that has led many to believe that the Queen actually had a pet ferret. Artistic licence is also thought to have been employed by the artist in the painting of this portrait because the creature has dark speckling in its coat. This colouration is thought to be unlikely to have been natural, and most likely was added by the artist to emulate the dark specks that appeared in the ermine fur collars of robes worn by the nobility. These black specks, as a matter of interest, when present in the ermine trim of robes, are in fact the black tips from stoat tails that have been skilfully incorporated by the furrier during the manufacture of the trimming for the robe.

Moving swiftly forward in time now, we come nearer to the present day. In 2001 the European Parliament passed legislation that allowed pets to travel with their owners within the European Union, subject to disease testing and inoculations. The documentation that was generated subsequent to the necessary requirements being met and served to prove such was called a 'pet passport'. However, in its first incarnation, it only applied to pets such as cats, dogs, hamsters, rabbits and guinea pigs. Ferrets were initially omitted from the ruling.

A protest was organized by *Ferret World* magazine and subsequently, on 10 April 2003, the European Parliament ruled that ferrets too could be issued with the same pet passport. This therefore enabled ferrets to travel abroad with their owners. In an article

The 'Ermine Portrait'. Courtesy of The Marquess of Salisbury

printed in the *Daily Mirror* newspaper at the time, a Liberal Democrat spokesman was quoted as saying, 'This law will make it easier for British males to breed with French females. It could have implications for the future of our breeding stock.' The same article stated that there were at the time of writing two million British ferret owners.

Nowadays, ferrets are firmly entrenched in their place with us. They have a number of uses or purposes, not least the most obvious role in which they first found themselves allied with mankind, that of being in the fields hunting rabbits and destroying other pest species. This is an application that I have already dealt with comprehensively in another book, *Ferrets and Ferreting* (also published by The Crowood Press; ISBN reference: 1-86126-564-6).

For many years the ferret has been quite important in the fur trade, its fur being called fitch. This is not surprising when you stop and remember that it is a close relative of the much-prized mink. In fact, many mustelid species were sought after for their fur until relatively recently, although this demand is now in demise due to the change in fashions.

The next most obvious role for ferrets is companionship. According to some sources, ferrets now rank in third place, behind cats and dogs in the list of most popular pet species in Europe and the United States of America, where, I might add as a point of interest, a ferret by the name of Pokey was actually given the office of mascot of the Colonial Navy of Massachusetts in a ceremony at Bristol Community College on 14 September 1986. The popularity of ferrets in the role of companionship should not be at all surprising to anyone who has encountered well-kept ferrets, as they are exceptionally clean, highly intelligent, amiable and friendly to those who care for them properly.

Ferrets are also popular entertainment at country shows. These entertainments being, for example, ferret racing, ferret-in-the-bin and fancy ferret shows.

In ferret racing, several pipes or tubes are laid out and numbered. People place a small wager or buy a ticket for their chosen number, and when all is ready a ferret is entered into one end of each pipe. Not surprisingly, the first ferret to reach the other end of its given pipe determines the winner.

Ferret-in-the-bin is a different proposition. A bin or barrel stands on the ground. It has several pipes protruding from it and each is numbered. Again, people place a small wager or buy a ticket for a particular numbered pipe. A ferret is placed in the bin, and whichever pipe it chooses to use to facilitate its exit from the bin determines the winner.

Fancy ferret shows are self-explanatory, although there are strict rules governing colour categories at more serious events held by clubs and organizations. During my research for this book I wrote to the National Ferret School for information relating to these regulations, but they declined to reply. Therefore, as a result of this I am having to use the information that I have obtained from the American Ferret Association via their website relating to colour standards. I doubt if there are many great differences, or at least I hope not! This information will be detailed in Chapter 8.

Another 'entertainment' or 'sport' that was practised until it was banned relatively recently due to pressure from animal welfare organizations because of the undue stress imposed on the ferrets involved was 'ferret legging'. There were even championships held for this pursuit, and the rules required that the ferrets used must each have a full set of teeth and be subject to no restraints. The human 'contender' was not permitted to wear any undergarments. This activity involved the person placing a ferret inside their trousers, and the competitor who could retain it within for the longest period of time was adjudged the winner. As previously stated, it was banned recently, but prior to this occurrence the record was held by a Yorkshireman of seventy-two years of age, with a duration of nearly five and a half hours!

The general belief is that this activity was probably originally born out of necessity, when poachers, not wishing to make it common knowledge that they were in possession of a ferret, had to secrete it about their person. It is thought that the trouser legs therefore provided the best hiding place, as they afforded the ferret reasonable space and kept it warm, and as a consequence the pockets were kept free for the carrying of nets and other traps such as snares and the like.

A further application or employment of the ferret's services may be surprising to some because it is in industry. Some contractors, I believe in the backstage or support in theatres, use ferrets in their occupation. If a cable, or number thereof, is required to be routed through a conduit or trunking, then a harness is fitted to a ferret. A string or cord is attached to the harness, and the ferret entered into one end of the channel. The ferret then makes its way to the other end, pulling the string along as it goes. When the ferret gets out at the other end, the string is detached from the harness, the cable or cables are attached to one end of the string, and are then pulled through with it to the other end. As a point of historical interest, the television cables for the broadcast of the wedding of Charles, the Prince of Wales, to Lady Diana Spencer in 1981 were installed in this manner.

A further use to which ferrets have been put, sadly I might add from my own point of view, is in laboratories in research into cures for the common cold and influenza. This is because the ferret is highly susceptible to these diseases and they are easily passed from human to ferret, and ferret to human, and so ferrets make excellent test subjects for the purposes of experimentation. They are also used for laboratory research in many other fields.

3

Anatomy and Physiology

SEXUAL DIMORPHISM

The first point to mention is that ferrets differ significantly in size relative to gender. That is to say, one sex is larger than the other. This is a phenomenon called sexual dimorphism. It is seen in many species, not just ferrets; however, mustelids are probably the most sexually dimorphic living mammals with the exception of pinnipeds.

In the case of ferrets, the hob (male) is, on average, approximately two to three times the size of the jill (female). Obviously, as with all things in nature, this is not always the case as every ferret is an individual. Some jills may be particularly large, and by the same token some hobs may be particularly small. But, if the two specimens being compared are from the same litter, or parentage, and have had the benefit of the same, or comparable, conditions throughout their development, then the resultant size differential is the most likely to be apparent.

The reason for sexual dimorphism has mystified scientists throughout time. The most obvious and least complicated possibility is related to food. Prey species of different-sized predators

Sexual dimorphism: hob (left) and jill (right). These two ferrets are litter siblings.

equally vary in size. That is to say that the male, being greater in size, is able to take larger prey, and so there is no need for competition for food between the genders. Also the female, being smaller, is able to hunt in smaller environments than the male can access, this being of the greatest benefit to her when she is in kindle or during the nursing of a litter of kittens. A further consideration is that a smaller body requires less nutrition to sustain it than a larger one, therefore, again when in kindle or nursing her young, the female will have greater reserves available to support her offspring from a given meal without suffering the ravages of malnutrition herself.

Another possibility is that males, being promiscuous, are in competition with each other for females at mating time. Obviously the largest and most dominant individual will have greater success and will mate with more females, thereby facilitating the survival of the fittest and, consequently, the largest.

SKELETAL STRUCTURE

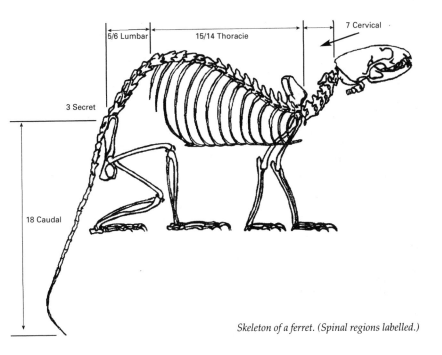

Skeleton of a ferret. (Spinal regions labelled.)

Mammalian skeletons are largely the same, although, if you examine carefully for variations in the skeletal structure between ferrets and other mammals, you will discover that some of the vertebrae of the spinal column are longer in the ferret pro rata to other mammals. This is particularly apparent in the neck or cervical region. Other areas that differ are that the limbs are shorter, again pro rata, than in most mammals and the skull is significantly elongated. In addition to these more obvious differences, it should also be noted that the jaw is effectively interlocked into the skull, allowing for a very powerful biting force.

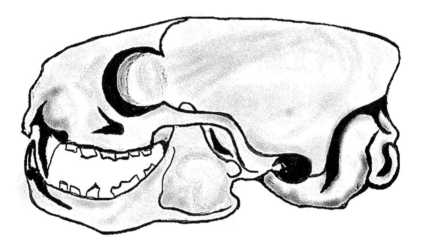

The skull of a ferret.

The ridges of the sagittal crest (skull top) and the occipital and nuchal crests (back of the skull) of the ferret are markedly pronounced. They also have a bony covering over the middle ear to afford it protection and improve hearing; this structure is called the auditory bulla.

The bones of the arms, or forelegs if you prefer, of a ferret, that is to say the humerus, radius and ulna, and the scapula of the shoulder, are relatively similar to our own, although the clavicle is not always found. When the clavicle is located, it is in the form of a small ossification in the muscle. The elbow differs from our own in that it has an extension to strengthen the limb for the purposes of digging.

The carpals, metacarpals and phalanges (bones of the hands) are almost identical to ours, with the exception of the third phalanx, which, as a necessity to support the nail, has a claw-like process. The claws or nails are permanently extended due to the fact that they are non-retractable.

The bones of the hind legs, the tibia, fibula and femur, again are comparable in shape to our own, allowing for the obvious size differential. There is a slight difference to the ankle bones, however, and the angle and position of tendon attachments differ slightly from our own.

One result of these differences is that the ferret's jumping ability is greatly enhanced, and another is that these short limbs facilitate access to small tunnels and underground workings, where, once they are in this environment, ferrets are very adaptable. The most obvious end result of these musculo-skeletal differences is that mustelids, and therefore ferrets, are amongst the strongest animals, weight for weight, on Earth. They are also most adept at digging, running and climbing.

Like us, ferrets have seven cervical vertebrae (the spinal bones of the neck), although they are, as previously stated, proportionally longer pro rata than our own. Their thoracic spine (the distance between the base of the neck and the top of the lumbar, or lower back, region) differs from ours in that ferrets have fifteen vertebrae, and consequently thirty ribs, although in some cases only fourteen vertebrae and twenty-eight ribs. The sternum (breast bone) is constructed of eight bones. Ferrets have either five or six lumbar (lower back) and three sacral vertebrae (the section of the spine between the bottom of the lumbar region and the sacroiliac joint, which is the juncture between the spine and the ilium or pelvis). An obviously major difference to us is that ferrets have eighteen caudal vertebrae to our three or four. We do not need them, as we have no tail!

The product of longer vertebrae, an elongated skull and shorter limbs is a predator that can manoeuvre magnificently in tunnels and other arenas where space is restricted or at least at a premium. This superb manoeuvrability allows the ferret to catch and kill its prey, which is often larger than itself, and, once having done this, be able to carry off the victim without tripping over it.

This ability of being able to catch, kill and carry larger prey species than itself is a most useful attribute, especially in the case of a jill with a hungry litter of kittens to feed. In this instance, one large victim will be sufficient to feed all, instead of her having to make multiple trips and risk multiple encounters, not only with her prey species but also with other creatures that may prey upon her.

An albino jill ferret preparing to make a leap.

In addition to being very flexible, the structure of a mustelid's vertebral column and its associated musculature affords the animal vast amounts of power relative to its size and weight.

In summation then, ferrets can run at what can only be described as amazing speeds, change direction incredibly efficiently whilst running, carry loads in excess of three times their own body weight, and many can jump distances of up to, and in excess of, four times their body length. None of which are mean feats by anyone's standards!

Shown above is an albino jill ferret preparing to make a leap. The leap in this case was one in which she increased her elevation (jumped upwards) in the order of approximately 10in (25.5cm) and travelled laterally (forwards horizontally) approximately 3ft (91cm). Her body length, excluding her tail, was approximately 8.5in (22cm).

EYES AND VISION

The basic structure of the eyes of the ferret is similar to that of all mammals. The pupil (the black 'window' of the eye) is round when fully dilated or opened in low-light situations, but it closes down as the light levels increase, into a slit in the case of the ferret. The reason for the slit closure is that the retina of the eye (the light-sensitive area at the back of the eye) is so sensitive that a round, or sphincter-like closure such as ours, would not allow the pupillary closure to be efficient enough at reducing the light levels reaching the retina, whereas the slit is. Ferrets have a sclera (the white part) just as we do, but this is not normally visible because it is protected behind the eyelids.

The eyes are muscled and the ferret can turn them independently of its head, and they move in conjunction with each other, as ours do. Due to the predatory nature of the ferret's existence, the eyes predominantly point in a forward-facing direction; however, as they are also prey to other species the eyes bulge outward from the head for a wider view of their surroundings.

The sensitivity of an eye is dependent on its ability to summarize the responses of its receptors. None of these individual responses is of sufficient intensity to cause an impulse in an optic nerve fibre. Eyes that have high levels of sensitivity do not have high acuity, or power of resolution. The visual acuity of an eye is dependent on its capability to distinguish the activity of one receptor from that of another. It is therefore interesting to note that the sensitivity of the eyes of a ferret compares almost identically with that of a cat's eyes, which are vastly more sensitive than a human's. However, as a result of this, the power of resolution is correspondingly less.

The retinal construction within the eye consists of cones for visualizing colours, and rods for grey tones. Ferret eyes have very few cones, but a high density of rods. They can clearly distinguish and discriminate red and blue from grey tones, but have only a slight sensitivity to yellow and green.

They have a layer at the rear of the retina that reflects light forwards; this is what makes their eyes appear to glow in the dark. It also bounces the available light in a way that causes the light photons to be able to stimulate the rods more than once. This therefore greatly enhances a ferret's ability to see in low-light situations, or, indeed, in the dark.

The visual capabilities of the ferret are exceptionally good when the viewed subject is close to, but, as the distance increases, so the acuity decreases. However, ferrets are most adept at noticing movement, particularly in shadows. These characteristics are largely due to the construction of the lens, and are ideally suited to the purpose of hunting prey in tunnels and subterranean workings.

Having considered the above, it should be noted that the ferret relies most significantly on its ears, nose and whiskers for sensory input from its surroundings.

ORAL STRUCTURE

Orally, ferrets have nine hyoid bones (bones at the base of the tongue). Their jaws do not fuse in the centre, and their upper incisors are rooted in premaxillary bones. The mandible, or jaw, joins approximately halfway down the skull, and the pre- and post-glenoid processes are enlarged and so developed that they effectively lock the lower mandible into the skull at the point of its articulation.

This largely precludes the type of chewing performed by herbivores, forcing the ferret to cut up its food into chunks and swallow it as such, which it does with its carnassial teeth. However, it also prevents the jaw from dislocating when opened wide to bite large animals, or indeed from the sheer strength of the bite, thereby facilitating an extremely powerful bite.

The majority of the muscular effort required for such a powerful bite is provided by the highly developed temporalis muscle (the muscle on the outside of the face that operates the jaw), the greatest development of muscular tissue having occurred in the posterior fibres of this muscle. The directions in which the anterior and posterior temporalis muscle fibres operate to exert the forces required in biting are shown in the illustration.

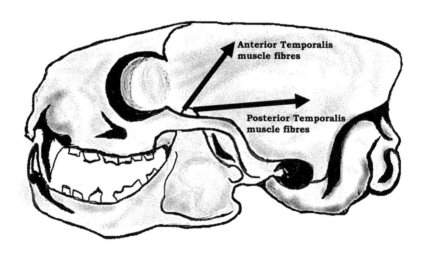

The skull of a ferret showing the direction of attachments of the temporalis muscle.

The anterior temporalis muscle fibres do most of the work when the jaw is opened wide, and the posterior temporalis muscle fibres are worked hardest when the jaw is almost closed as the carnassial teeth bite off pieces of food or crunch bone. As a result of this, there has to be an exaggeration of the normal progressive transition of use from anterior to posterior temporalis muscle fibres as the jaw closes. This arrangement of the musculature also greatly increases the torque exerted at the point of articulation, which goes some way to explaining the degree of development of the pre- and post-glenoid processes.

Some believe the bite of a ferret to be the most powerful, weight for weight, of all carnivores. A biting capability such as this therefore is a most useful attribute for a creature who often encounters and kills prey much larger than itself, not to mention its defensive value if attacked by another predator looking for food.

DENTITION

Ferrets, like us, develop two sets of teeth, the first being deciduous and the second permanent. The deciduous teeth begin erupting at about twenty-one to twenty-eight days of age and can number up to thirty teeth; firstly the four canines, followed usually by the incisors, which number in the order of twelve to fourteen teeth. The next to erupt are the third and fourth premolars, followed by the second premolar.

The thirty-four permanent teeth erupt between about fifty and seventy-four days of age. The order is as follows; timings, as with anything in nature, are approximate:

- fifty days – upper and lower canines; first molar
- fifty-three days – upper first molar
- sixty days – upper second, third and fourth premolars; lower second premolar
- sixty-seven days – lower third premolar
- seventy-four days – lower fourth premolar; second molar.

The sequence can vary according to genetics, nutrition and the general health of the ferret.

Premolars normally are subsequent to the eruption of first molars. Permanent molars form beneath the deciduous teeth, but the canines and incisors form adjacent to their predecessors.

uous teeth are not lost until the permanent teeth have almost erupted, meaning that kittens can be weaned onto solid food at an early age, as they can continue to feed themselves from provided food whilst shedding their deciduous teeth.

Carnassial teeth are the upper third premolar and lower first molar, and are intended for cutting through tissues and bone, but they also crunch cereal and other foods.

GASTROENTEROLOGY

Ferrets are subject to olfactory imprinting, which means that whatever is fed to them during the first six months of their lives is recognized as food. The digestive system of the ferret is very short; typically food will pass through in a period of three to five hours.

They have neither caecum (the small sac that is present at the juncture of the large and small bowels in some species), nor appendix (a protrusion from the caecum that is used mainly by herbivores) at the juncture between the large and small bowels. The distinction between the large and small bowels is not visually apparent at their juncture in ferrets, and this is not at all unusual in predominantly carnivorous species.

OTHER GLANDS

Other interesting points are that ferrets have musk or scent glands, from which, if frightened, they emit a strong-smelling foul odour as a defence mechanism. These consist of two groups of modified skin glands that each empty into a storage sac, which in turn empties via a sphincter into the rectum approximal to the anus.

The discharge of the sacs is controlled voluntarily. The resulting secretion, the musk, is a thick, oily, yellow fluid that has a very powerful smell. In addition to its use as a defence mechanism, a little musk is passed with faeces and serves to mark territories.

Ferrets have no sweat glands and are therefore incapable of sweating, despite the term 'the sweats' being erroneously applied in the case of a ferret suffering from heatstroke.

Also it should be noted that the male ferret has no prostate gland, and therefore cannot control the flow of urine from the bladder. Kittens have apocrine glands on their necks in order that the jill can discriminate between her young and food when carrying them. This helps to prevent unintentional cannibalism due to her making this fateful mistake, because she can be quite highly stressed by the workloads on her when she continually has to return the kittens to the nest once they are able to move around.

REPRODUCTION

The male ferret has spines on the outside of its penis, called penial spines. It also has a bone in its penis called a baculum, or os penis. This bone is similar to that of a close relative, *Mustela nivalis*, the weasel. The penial spines are thought either to aid in the retention of the penis within the vulva, or to assist in the stimulation required to induce the female to ovulate during the act of coitus, or possibly both.

The presence of the baculum facilitates extended mating sessions, which can and often do last for hours. Hammond and Marshall recorded the longest act of coitus that I can find on record in 1930, and it lasted for 180 minutes, or three hours.

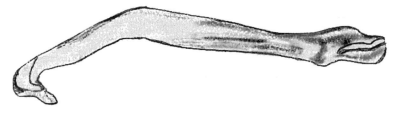

The baculum of Mustela nivalis.

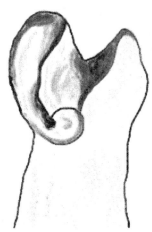

The distal end of a baculum.

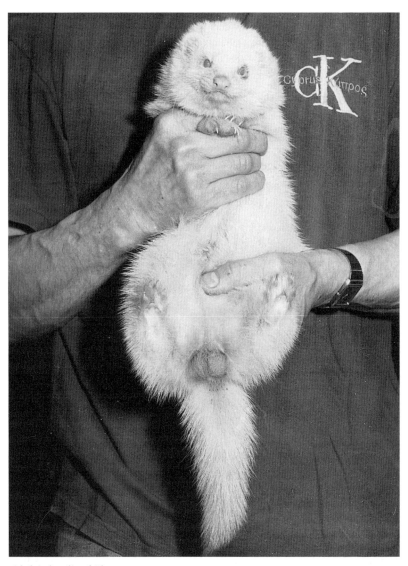

A hob in breeding fettle.

Ferrets are photoperiodic; that is to say, they will come into season, or breeding fettle, and out again at the behest of nature as the daylight hours increase and decrease. As spring approaches and the hours of daylight increase, hobs, the male of the species, will come into breeding fettle. Their testicles will descend from within the abdominal cavity into the scrotum and swell. The scrotum will enlarge to facilitate this.

Similarly, but usually slightly later than hobs, jills will come into oestrus. Their vulva, the tissue surrounding the vaginal orifice, will swell and distend from the body of the animal by about a centimetre or possibly more. This distension will be complete, and therefore maximized, about ten to fourteen days after its initiation.

A jill in season.

At the end of the breeding season, and as the hours of daylight decrease, a hob's testicles will reduce in size and be retracted back up into the abdominal cavity. His scrotum will also shrink.

A jill, if still in season at this time, will come out of oestrus, or regress. Her vulva will revert to its pre-oestrus normal condition, which is as a regular orifice situated just below the anus, with no distension.

When a jill is in season she must be taken out of oestrus or her health will be seriously affected. This can be achieved in a number of ways:

- She can be taken to a vet and given an injection of hormones (a 'jill jab').
- She can be served by a hoblet (vasectomized hob).
- She can be mated with a hob.

The first option is an injection of hormones that simulates her hormonal balance during pregnancy. This causes her body to believe that she is in kindle, and thereby it regresses from oestrus, consequently protecting her health.

The second option results in her being induced to ovulate as she would do naturally, had she been mated with a complete hob. She will again regress from oestrus, but because the hoblet is sterile pregnancy will not result. Her health will again be protected.

Prior to the coupling, the jill's vulva will be moist. Often the area surrounding the vulva, outward to her hind legs, and forward by approximately 2cm or sometimes more, will be wet. Usually within about three days post-coitus this area, including the vulva, will dry out. This is thought to be an indication that ovulation has been stimulated. Therefore, as a result of this she will regress from oestrus, and her health will be protected from the complications associated with prolonged oestrus.

Both of the first two options can and do carry the risk of other health problems, such as pyometra, or other infections, and therefore particular attention should be paid to monitoring her condition carefully. The third option should result in pregnancy, and she will regress from oestrus as a result.

A fourth option available to keepers to protect a jill's health, that is obviously only an option should they never wish to breed from her, is to have her neutered or spayed as soon as she is old enough.

This action is an invasive surgical procedure that excises her reproductive organs, the uterus and the ovaries; it consequently sterilizes

A hoblet, displaying the two abdominal scars left by the bilateral incisions that were necessary to carry out the sterilization procedure.

her and prevents her from being able to conceive. It also means that she will never come into oestrus, thereby negating the health risks associated with her remaining in prolonged oestrus.

To be able to exercise the second of the above options, the services of a hoblet are obviously required. A hoblet is the term or name given to a hob ferret that has been vasectomized.

This again is an invasive surgical procedure, and should only be performed by a qualified veterinary surgeon when the candidate is fully in breeding fettle, that is to say his testicles are fully descended into his scrotum. Surgical incision(s) are made into the abdomen, then the vas deferens, the tubes that carry the sperm between the testicles and the seminal vesicle in a complete male, are located by the surgeon, who then ligates and separates them, at the same time removing a short length from each of them to prevent them from reattaching or reconnecting themselves.

This action thereby results in the subject being sterilized. He will, however, still have the desire to copulate, and be capable of doing so, but as a result of his sterilization he will be incapable of impregnating the female.

The above procedure should not be confused with the castration of a hob ferret, such procedure resulting in him then being called a hobble.

This procedure involves the removal of both of his testicles, which will obviously sterilize him, but he will no longer have the desire or the ability to copulate, thereby rendering him useless should he be required to remove a jill from oestrus.

The above situations having been taken into consideration, should you wish to breed you must obviously use a pair of, ideally, complete ferrets. I say ideally because should either one or even both have had to have either one testicle or one ovary removed for medical reasons, they are still fertile and still capable of breeding, although their fertility will have been adversely affected.

SUMMARY

Chromosomes:	forty (in twenty pairs)
Temperature:	38.6°C / 101.5°F
Pulse/heart rate:	230 +/− 20 beats per minute (BPM)
Respiratory rate:	thirty to forty breaths per minute
Mammary glands:	eight, male and female (the female is the only gender capable of lactation)
Litter size:	up to fifteen
Birth weight:	0.3oz +/−0.18oz (10g +/−5g)
Birth status:	blind, deaf and naked
Open ears and eyes:	twenty-one to thirty-five days
Fur:	within seven days
Teeth:	
Deciduous:	twenty-one days onwards
Permanent:	fifty days onwards
Ovulation:	approx. thirty hours post-coitus
Gestation:	forty-two days
Weaning:	eight weeks
Separation/sale:	twelve weeks

4

Genetics

Genetics is the study of the genes, the word 'gene' being derived from 'genesis', meaning 'the beginning'. It is the branch of biology that deals with heredity and variation; the inherited characteristics of an organism, in this case the ferret. It is a subject that is avoided by many, possibly out of fear of the unknown, but need not be unnecessarily overcomplicated. Deep specialist knowledge in the field of zoological science is certainly not required, although some technical terms will probably need to be learned and remembered. Once the basics in the form of some fundamental rules and principles are also learned, provided that common sense is employed, the subject can become quite logical and straightforward.

If anyone is considering breeding an animal, I believe it is good practice to at least make the effort to gain, as a minimum, a basic working knowledge of genetics. There is an old saying, 'put the best to the best, and hope for the best'. Whilst, fundamentally speaking, this has some value, any breeding entered into on this premise will be haphazard to say the least. It is far better to have some knowledge and understanding of genetics with which to work. There is also a benefit on a personal level in that you will have a greater sense of achievement when the required progeny are produced as planned.

THE BEGINNING OF GENETICS

So, to the background of genetics: an Augustinian monk by the name of Gregor Mendel carried out early studies in the field of genetics. In 1866 Mendel, a trained scientist and teacher of maths, was experimenting with growing peas as he did not believe that genetic inheritance was a result of blending. His basis for this belief was that from hybrid strains of his own production the original parental variations would sometimes re-emerge, unchanged, in later generations. (The term 'throwback' is now used to describe this occurrence.) If the hybrids that he had produced in earlier experiments were simply mixtures of their parental stock, the re-emergence of the originals would not have been possible.

He hypothesized that the passing on of individual particles controlled inheritance. He called these particles 'factors', but we now call them genes. He said that these genes control the characteristics of an individual, and each individual has two for each characteristic, one being supplied by each parent. From this work he was able to predict the outcome of the crossing of two pure strains of peas.

He described the resulting characteristics of the hybrid in terms of dominant and recessive genes. These terms are still in use to this day, as is his notation, whereby he used, and we still use, upper-case letters for dominant and lower-case letters for recessive genes.

These findings, along with the supporting evidence, were originally published in the *Proceedings of the Natural History Society of Brno* and were not known of outside of the Society's small membership until thirty-four years later in the year 1900, when a Dutch botanist by the name of de Vries came across the paper and republished it, ensuring that the credit for the theory remained with Mendel, its originator.

DNA

The actual genetic structure of any living thing is called 'the genome'. It contains, and is made up of, the genes. Genes actually exert their influence by directing the production of enzymes and proteins. This, in turn, facilitates chemical reactions within the cell. George W. Beadle and L. Tatum of the USA demonstrated this in the 1940s.

The chromosomal component that carries genetic information was found to be deoxyribonucleic acid (DNA) and shown as such in 1944 by Oswald T. Avery. However, it was not until 1953 that James D. Watson of the USA and Francis H. C. Crick of Great Britain, both working on the problem in Cambridge, deduced its molecular structure.

Later, in 1961, two French geneticists, François Jacob and Jacques Monod, discovered the process by which DNA actually directs the protein synthesis in bacterial cells. These developments, in turn, led to the DNA molecule's genetic code being deciphered, and, ultimately, to the techniques that exist today in the field of genetic engineering.

The DNA controls the continuous production of proteins throughout the entire body, and is essentially the basis of how a living thing works, whether it is a plant, an animal, or any other form of life. It is also the blueprint, for want of a better term, of each individual, and therefore the vehicle that carries that individual's genetic code on to the next generation.

To delve any more deeply into the structure of DNA and genetic engineering within this text would, I feel, be superfluous to our requirements. If further information is desired, there are texts available that are written by specialists in that particular field.

GENETIC CODE

So, to begin at the most elementary level it must always be remembered that any progeny, or offspring if you prefer, inherits half of its traits and attributes from each parent. On occasions, it may appear that more is inherited from one parent than another. This, however, is not so. With ferrets, as with all life as we know it, the characteristics of any offspring are defined by the chromosomes passed by the parents at the time of fertilization.

Each parent supplies one half of the genetic code as chromosomes in the form of sperm or ovum/egg, these being called the gametes. DNA has been shown to be in the form of a double helix; a gamete is half of the double helix, one string of the chromosome pairs. When combined at the moment of fertilization they produce the zygote, forming a new double helix of DNA (one half from each parent) and the beginning of the new individual.

Chromosome strings are always of an equal number and can therefore be classified as chromosome pairs. Early studies on these pairs soon discovered that not all of them were exact pairs. In female animals, all pairs were matched. However, in the male animals the chromosomes in one pair were not exactly the same. It was soon realized that these were the sex chromosomes, and therefore it is thought to be the father's contribution that defines the sex of the offspring.

THE QUESTION OF SEX

The sex chromosomes were designated X and Y. The female has an XX pair, and the male has an XY pair. When the female produces ova, or eggs, the genetic code carried within each is produced as an exact copy of one of the strings of her DNA; consequently they have a single X chromosome.

When the male produces sperm the genetic code carried by them is again formed as an exact copy of one of the strings of his DNA. However, because one string of his DNA has an X chromosome, and the other a Y chromosome for the sex pair, the total sperm formed are half carrying an X and half carrying a Y chromosome. Consequently, by virtue of this fact, it is thought that the sex of the offspring is entirely dependent on whether the egg is fertilized by a sperm carrying an X or a Y chromosome.

MUTATION AND EVOLUTION

The evolution of a species is as a result of a process called 'mutation'. This phrase was coined by its discoverer, H. J. Muller, from the Latin for 'change'. Muller was an American geneticist, and he made his discovery in 1915.

He was working on breeding experiments when he noticed that on occasions a completely new allele (a variant form of a gene) would emerge. This allele should not have been present, as it could not have been inherited from either parent. He realized that this was as a result of a chemical change within the subject. He followed this event through to find that after this initial mutation has occurred, the allele is inherited in its new form in the normal way on subsequent occasions; it does not revert to its original self. This, he deduced, was the source of genetic variation – of evolution.

COLOUR BREEDING

The ferret has forty chromosomes, or twenty pairs. As previously stated, there are two types of characteristic carried by the genes within the chromosomes, dominant and recessive. Whilst all of the characteristics of each individual are controlled by these factors, I am not aware of any detailed studies of the whole genome being carried out with reference to ferrets, therefore the genetics dealt with within this chapter will be restricted to colour variation and inheritance.

With this reference to colour and its variation, a dominant characteristic is visually apparent, or, to term it correctly, phenotypical, and a recessive one not so. As previously stated, in genetic 'shorthand' a dominant gene of a given pair is represented by an upper-case letter, or capital, and a recessive one by a lower-case letter. Two of these genes, that is to say one pair, are related to the colour of the animal concerned.

Each animal, having two colour genes, is therefore represented by two letters, one for each gene. If both colour genes are the same, the animal is said to be pure-bred. If the letters are mixed it is said to be a split. The letters used in the following examples are 'P' for polecat colouring and 'a' for albino. The 'P' will always be upper case, because, being the natural colouration, should the polecat colour gene be present, it is always the dominant of the two genes and therefore the animal concerned will always be phenotypically of polecat colouration.

The 'a' will always be lower case because it is always recessive. Even in the case of pure albino colouration, that is, the total absence of any colour pigment, the 'a' will always be shown in lower case in both representational letters.

A polecat-coloured ferret.

An albino-coloured ferret.

Beyond, or should I say in-between, these two opposite ends of possible colour variation, there is also the sandy-coloured ferret. If present in a phenotypically polecat-coloured ferret, the sandy gene will be 'masked', that is, it will be recessive and consequently represented by a lower-case letter. If it is present with an albino colour gene, it will mask the albino gene, producing a ferret that is phenotypically sandy in colouration. In this instance, the sandy gene will be dominant; consequently, it will be represented by an upper-case letter.

A sandy-coloured ferret.

Having given the explanation of how the colour inheritance works genetically, the easiest way to describe the above for ease of committal to memory is to say that, if the polecat gene is present, it will *always* mask all other colours. If the polecat colour gene is absent, and the sandy colour gene is present, it will take the next level of precedence, masking out the albino gene. Whenever the albino gene is present, it will *always* be recessive, due to the lack of colour pigmentation.

Male genes
(pure polecat)

	P	P
P	PP	PP
P	PP	PP

Female genes
(pure polecat)

An example of a Punnett Square for a pure polecat pairing.

This type of genetic colour notation is generally presented graphically in a table. This table is called a Punnett Square and an example is shown above.

The Punnett Square here shows the projected outcome of breeding from a pair of pure polecat-coloured ferrets. The male genes are on the top edge, and the female on the left side. The genetic make-up of the progeny, in percentage or fractional terms, is shown in the remaining boxes of the square.

It can be clearly seen that dominant genes from both parents result in the progeny having a pair of dominant genes. Therefore they should have a polecat phenotype; however, it is possible for a mutation to occur, producing a variant in any or all of the progeny. This possibility is always a potential occurrence in any pairing.

Should the pairing have taken the form of a pair of ferrets that were both albino, then a lower-case letter 'a' would need to be substituted for each of the parent's genetic representational letters. From this, it follows that the result would be a litter of all albino progeny.

Naturally, it also follows that should the pairing have been between a pair of pure sandy ferrets, then by the same token the resultant progeny would be pure sandy.

Male genes
(pure polecat)

	P	P
a	Pa	Pa
a	Pa	Pa

Female genes
(pure albino)

A Punnett Square for a pairing of a pure polecat and a pure albino.

As can be seen from this diagram, despite both parents being purebred, and both possessing pairs of dominant genes for their phenotype, the resulting progeny will be expected to be of a polecat phenotype, with recessive albino genes.

The progeny of this pairing are termed 'splits'. As previously stated, this is due to the fact that even though the albino genes were dominant in one of the parents (this being due to the absence of any other colour genes in this parent), once paired with the polecat genes in the zygote that resulted from the coupling of the gametes carrying the relevant genes from each parent, they became recessive due to the dominance of the polecat gene taking precedence, as a result of its being the natural colour and having colour pigment. A less complicated way of explaining this, having given the full explanation above, that may make it easier to understand would be to say that the polecat gene 'masks' out the albino gene.

As mentioned above, the polecat colouring or markings, being the 'natural' or normal colour, will always dominate if present. Therefore, phenotypically speaking, if the polecat colour gene is present the animal will be polecat-coloured.

The only time that an animal's phenotype will correspond to a recessive colour gene is if both of its colour genes are recessive. This is only so in the case of albinos.

In addition to this, the only times that the progeny of a pairing will have an albino phenotype is if it is the progeny of a pure albino pairing, or if both genes are recessive albino: the result of a pairing of two splits whose recessive genes are albino. This will always be the case in the normal run of events; however, it may be possible for an albino to be produced unexpectedly if a mutation should occur or if there is a total breakdown of the colour genes from a coloured parent pairing.

Male genes
(split)

Female genes
(split)

	P	a
P	PP	Pa
a	Pa	aa

A Punnett Square for the pairing of a pair of polecat/albino splits.

Illustrated here is the projected result of breeding from a pair of splits, that is, ferrets whose phenotype is polecat, but they carry the albino gene recessively.

The expected outcome of a pairing such as this is that 25 per cent of the litter will be pure polecat, carrying two dominant polecat genes; 50 per cent will be splits, phenotypically being polecat but carrying the albino gene recessively; and 25 per cent will be phenotypically, and pure, albino. These figures are commonly referred to as 1:2:1 or 25:50:25 to denote the ratio of the theoretical colour content of a given litter.

Male genes
(polecat / albino split)

	P	a
P	PP	Pa
s	Ps	Sa

Female genes
(polecat / sandy split)

A Punnett Square for a pairing of a polecat/albino split with a polecat/sandy split.

As can be seen from this Punnett Square, should the pairing take the form of a pair of splits that are one polecat / albino, and one polecat / sandy, then the expected progeny would be in the ratio of 25 per cent pure polecat, and 75 per cent splits, whose ratios would be in the order of approximately 66 per cent phenotypically polecat, of whom half would be with recessive albino genes, and half with recessive sandy genes. The remaining 25 per cent of the total progeny, and consequently approximately 33 per cent of the splits, would be phenotypically sandy in colouration, but with recessive albino genes.

Male genes
(sandy / albino split)

	S	a
P	Ps	Pa
a	Sa	aa

Female genes
(polecat / albino split)

A Punnett Square for the pairing of a sandy/albino split with a polecat/albino split.

This Punnett Square shows the expected result of a pairing between a sandy / albino split with a polecat / albino split. As can be seen, the only pure-colour progeny are pure albino, resulting from the combination of the recessive albino genes present in both parents. The remainder of the resultant progeny from this pairing are splits. Fifty per cent of the total progeny, and approximately 66 per cent of the splits, are phenotypically polecat-coloured, with half carrying the recessive sandy gene and half carrying the recessive albino gene. The remaining 25 per cent of the total progeny, and approximately 33 per cent of the splits, are phenotypically sandy in colouration with a recessive albino gene.

Should the pairing take the form of inbreeding between a split from a previous litter, and one of its parents that is recessive, the resulting progeny would be expected to be 50 per cent pure albino and 50 per cent splits. This is illustrated by the following diagram.

Male genes
(split kit)

Female genes (recessive parent)		P	a
a	Pa	aa
a	Pa	aa

A Punnett Square for the pairing of a polecat/albino split with a pure recessive albino.

Despite these tables and figures looking very impressive and accurate, it should be noted that to receive results exactly like these numerically speaking is highly unlikely, unless you are breeding huge numbers of animals.

Simple things that can render them inaccurate are occurrences such as an uneven number of kittens in a litter, or possibly only one kit being born! In the event that only one kit is produced, I would hope that it goes without saying that the litter is 100 per cent of the phenotype and genetic structure of the existing kit and 0 per cent of any other possible variants.

5

Breeding

The keeping of any species, whether it is for reasons of companionship or working purposes, is one thing; the next possible progression is to breed. However, the decision to breed is not one to be taken lightly and very careful consideration must be given to the motives behind the decision and its future implications, should you take the decision to proceed.

If the decision to breed has been made, it should be noted that the total novice, as when breeding any other species, should not attempt the breeding of ferrets. A reasonable depth of animal husbandry experience ought to be accrued.

The responsibility and commitment must also be understood, and accepted. It is not enough to think that the chosen pair will be mated and separated after the coupling, and the jill subsequently left to get on with the job of rearing the progeny. This type of approach or attitude is not only irresponsible and uncaring; it can also be detrimental, possibly even fatal, to the health of the dam and her kittens.

KEEPING RECORDS

For any breeding programme to be efficient and successful it must have one basically fundamental requirement – good record keeping. There are a number of possible methods:

- Notes in a loose-leaf pad. This is the most basic option, and whilst it will suffice, over time the pages may become damaged or lost, along with the vital, precious data on them.
- Card indexes. This, I feel, is an improvement on the last option, in that the medium employed is more resilient and will probably be marginally better protected. However, it is still susceptible to damage from wear or accident.
- Personal computer. This is my preferred option, as much data can be stored, and records printed off for use in the above methods if

required. I use Microsoft Access as I find it easy to use and efficient, although there are other options available. Whilst I believe that this is by far the most efficient and secure method of keeping records, it must be remembered always to back up any data or records on disk. This simple contingency plan will prove invaluable in case of problems such as a system failure or crash as you will not lose the stored information. It is also good practice and well worth the time to keep more than one copy of the back-up disks, stored securely and separately, so that in the case of a major problem such as the aforementioned failure or crash being compounded by the fact that a back-up disk has become corrupted in some way, the data are still not lost!

Whichever of the above methods is utilized, the information recorded should be as comprehensive as possible. Each pairing should have details such as: sire, sire colour, sire genetics, dam, dam colour, dam genetics, mating date, separation date (if the dam is usually kept communally with other jills), full-term due date, date of birth, litter size, litter notes. In addition to these basic details, it can be useful to

---

FERRET BREEDING RECORDS

SIRE

SIRE COLOUR

SIRE GENETICS

DAM

DAM COLOUR

DAM GENETICS

MATING DATE

DAM ISOLATED

F/T DUE DATE

BIRTH DATE

LITTER SIZE

LITTER NOTES

RETAINED ?

RETAINED DETAILS

RETAINED NAMES

An example of my ferret breeding report sheets.

Ferret Records

Name

Number

Sex

Colour

Genetics

Source

DOB

DOD

Sire

Sire Genetics

Dam

Dam Genetics

Medical History

Identichip No.

An example of my ferret records report sheets.

note if any of the litter were retained by you, and, if so, any details about them and their names. (Note: the genetics mentioned in the list relate only to colour genetics.)

If Access is used, it is also quite easy to create reports for each mating, so as to be able to print off hard copies of the information as required.

I also keep another set of records similar to this containing data relating to each individual ferret in my care. An additional entry, if you have your ferrets identichipped for security reasons, would naturally be the identichip number. If records are kept in this manner, the heredity, and the genetics thereof, can be traced back through parentage, grand-parentage, great-grand-parentage and so on, for any individual.

MATING

Once having selected the pair from whom you wish to breed, they must be examined for readiness. The hob's testicles should be fully descended into his scrotum for him to be fertile. Should his testicles not be fully descended, whilst he will be capable of carrying out the physical act of mating, he will be infertile. The jill's vulva should be fully distended or swollen (see the illustrations on p. 34 and p.35).

Assuming that the above is in order, the jill should be taken and introduced to the hob in his cage or cub. If the introduction is made in this manner then the jill will be on his territory and much more likely to be submissive. In all probability, within moments of the introduction, he will seize her by the scruff of her neck, drag her to a place of his choosing (this is commonly, but not always, the bed) and penetrate her.

The actual coupling may last for hours, and, if they are left together, in all likelihood will be repeated again and again for as long as they remain together. These repeated acts of coitus will be punctuated by short breaks in which they will probably sleep, and/or clean themselves and each other.

It should be noted that the mating process is very rough and in the course of the act the hob will treat his jill quite violently. During this time the jill's head may be seen or heard to impact on the cage sides or frame structure. Whilst you may be tempted to intervene on her behalf, you must not as the intensity and violence is necessary to induce ovulation, which will typically occur approximately thirty hours post-coitus.

After a period of hours (I personally would never allow the period to exceed twenty-four hours), the pair should be separated and inspected for damage. Particular attention should be given to the area around the jill's neck and ears. Should any damage be found it should be bathed with a saline solution and, if necessary, dusted with antiseptic wound powder.

POST-COITUS

The fact that the jill is stimulated to ovulate by the intensity and violence of the mating procedure means that there should be little chance of her not conceiving. Prior to mating, as well as the jill's vulva being swollen and distended, it will also usually be moist. It is also normal for the ano-genital region around the vulva, extending outward to her hind legs, and forward by 2cm or more along her stomach, to be wet.

Often by about three days post-coitus this area, including the vulva, will become dry. This is thought to be an indication that ovulation was

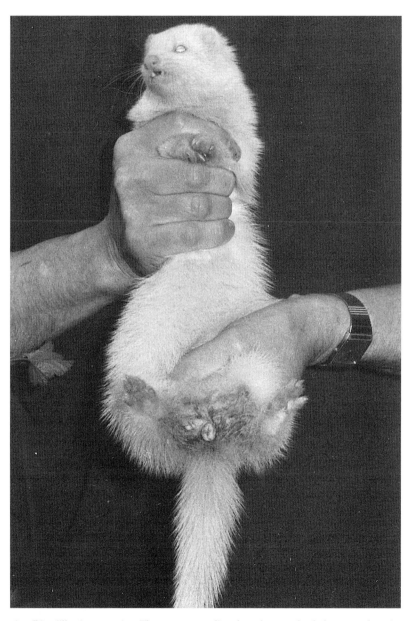

An albino jill prior to mating. The area surrounding the vulva can clearly be seen to be quite wet.

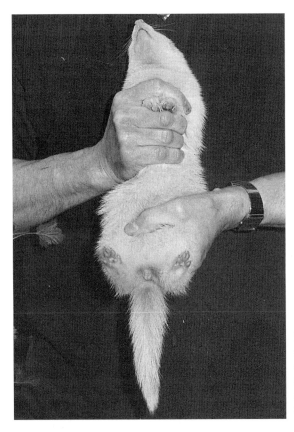

The same albino jill, five days post-coitus. The area surrounding the vulva, which was previously wet, can now clearly be seen to be dry.

indeed induced, and therefore the mating should have been successful.

The gestation period of ferrets is forty-two days, but a couple of days either side is not particularly unusual. The jill can be returned to her court, assuming she is kept communally, for the first four weeks of this time.

The swelling of her vulva should have begun to regress within about ten days, and she should have returned to her normal preoestrus appearance, that is without distension of the vulva, in around two to three weeks. It may be possible, with experience, to detect the presence of foetuses by gentle palpation of the abdomen from about three weeks or so post-coitus onwards.

Four weeks post-coitus the jill should be removed from her court and settled on her own in a large, suitable nursing cage, where she

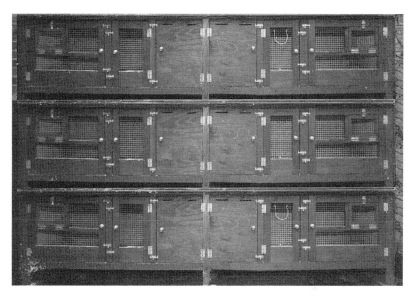

Breeding/nursing cages.

can build her nest and prepare for the birth, or, to term it correctly, parturition. I would hope that it goes without saying that a jill with a litter of kittens will require a significantly larger cage unit than a lone ferret so as to give her and her family adequate space to develop and grow.

As the kittens grow and become more mobile, even if the jill has had an average litter of six to eight, you will find it increasingly difficult to keep them in the cage when you are handling them or feeding and attending to your daily duties of cleaning and caring for them. However, despite the operational complications, under no circumstances should these essential duties of care be foregone.

Therefore, if you should construct your breeding and nursing units as per the diagram on p. 56, I would advise modifying the main door in a similar manner to include what I call a 'kit door' within the frame of the main door. It will not prevent older kittens from attempting escape, as they are incredibly adept at climbing, but you will have much more control. A close-up photograph of a modified main door is shown on p. 56, and a diagram of its construction is also shown. The wire mesh on all wire doors should be of weldmesh or twillweld, with holes of no greater than 0.5in (13mm) square.

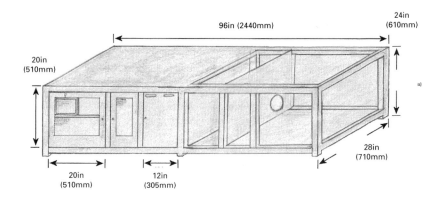

Diagram of a double breeding/nursing cage unit. The entry/exit hole between the bed and run is approximately 4in/100mm in diameter.

Close-up of a modified door.

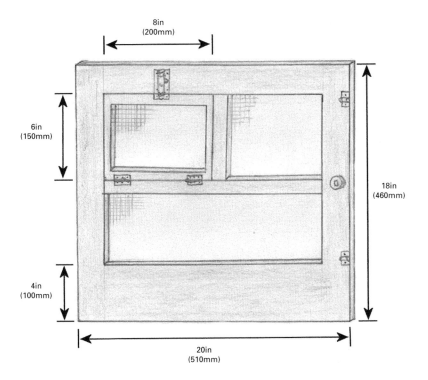

8in
(200mm)

6in
(150mm)

4in
(100mm)

18in
(460mm)

20in
(510mm)

Diagram of a modified door.

During the pregnancy, it is not unusual for the expectant mother to shed her guard hairs (the long coarse hairs), and be reduced to her soft, fine undercoat in the latter stages of her pregnancy. So, in the event that this should this occur, there is no cause for alarm. In fact, she may well use these hairs to line the inside of her nest.

Unless it is absolutely unavoidable, the jill should not be picked up or handled at all during the last three or four days of her pregnancy. It must be stressed that, especially during pregnancy, whenever a jill is handled particular attention must be given to supporting her hind quarters to prevent injury, specifically spinal injury, due to the increased abdominal weight being carried, and therefore suspended on her spine and associated musculature.

BIRTH AND REARING

At nature's behest, approximately forty-two days post-coitus, the pregnant jill will give birth. In my experience to date, the event will often take place either late at night or in the early hours of the morning. Ferrets are self-sufficient, and assuming there are no complications, she will need no assistance during the parturition and should be left to handle the event in peace. This having been said, assuming that you have a good relationship with her, it might be prudent to check her occasionally during the proceedings to ensure that all is well.

Should there be any apparent complications that are of concern, then the dam, along with any kittens born up to this point in time, and if possible her nest so as not to distress her any more than is absolutely unavoidable, should be taken to a veterinary surgeon without delay and professional advice sought.

The fact that in my experience to date parturition usually occurs either in the early hours of the day or late at night, but not in the heat of the middle of the day, I assume is possibly due to the lower ambient temperatures making the ordeal more bearable for her. However, the fact that this has been that which has occurred to date in my personal experience does not mean that it will always be so, nor is it necessarily always so.

The birth weight of the kittens is about 0.3oz (10g), and they are blind, deaf and naked, and totally dependent on their mother. Their number will probably be between one and fifteen, the average being six to eight. In dark-coloured kits their colour will generally begin to become apparent within eight to ten days.

In all cases, but particularly if she has a large litter, it will be beneficial to both the mother and her litter to go to her daily with a dish of lukewarm milk to help nourish her. This also serves to aid her in her production of milk for lactation. Once or twice per week an egg yolk can be beaten into it, to give extra nutritional support, but no more frequently as too much egg will overload her with certain vitamins that in too high a level can prove detrimental and, in extreme cases, fatal. In the interests of safety and hygiene you should always remain with her, holding the dish until she has taken all that she wants. It is important to do this to avoid the contents of the dish being spilt, which, should it occur, not only causes a mess in the cage, but also pollutes the environment giving rise to the possibility of either the dam or her kittens suffering food poisoning.

During lactation particular attention should be given to the inspection of her nipples to ensure that she does not develop mastitis. This is the inflammation of the mammary glands or nipples. Should this develop and be allowed to become severe, then the tissue may become gangrenous or necrotic and it will be necessary for the affected tissue to be excised surgically. The most likely times for this to occur are early in the rearing of the litter, or after the third week of lactation when the demand for milk by her litter increases substantially.

The kittens will suckle from her for in the region of four to six weeks, although they are capable of feeding themselves from the age of about three weeks. Whilst they are capable of feeding themselves from this early age, be warned, because if they should do so it may be an indication that the dam is unable to nourish them sufficiently well, and therefore there may be a problem that needs addressing with relevance to her health.

The demands placed upon her by the feeding and nurturing of her litter, not to mention the constant recovery of her kittens from their wanderings back to the nest, will often cause the mother to lose some of her general condition. In mild cases this is not a great concern, but should there be any marked or sudden deterioration in her condition the cause must be investigated and, if necessary, professional veterinary attention sought.

It should be noted here that ferret kittens have apocrine glands on their necks. These help the dam to differentiate between her kittens and food, and protect the family from accidental cannibalism due to the enormous stresses on her.

The handling of the kittens should begin as soon as possible to familiarize them with human hands and scent, but always rub your hands in the cage litter prior to handling them so as not to alarm the jill. In some case, the jill may have to be housed in a box throughout this process if she is over-protective.

Whilst handling the kittens dip your fingers in warmed milk or egg and milk mix and allow them to lick it from your skin. If any of them should nip or nibble tap them gently on the nose to dissuade the unwanted behaviour, but always finish with each kitten feeding from you not being chastised. This procedure should, if adhered to and carried out on a daily basis, produce good, easily handled ferrets.

Deciduous teeth will begin to erupt from about twenty-one days, permanent teeth from about fifty days of age. Their eyes and ears will open between twenty-one and thirty-five days of age. Ordinarily they will be weaned at around eight weeks of age, but they should not be separated from their mother any earlier than twelve weeks of age as they still have a lot to learn from her.

Birth in progress.

One day of age.

Three days of age.

Five days of age.

Seven days of age.

6
Nutritional Requirements

Protein	At least 30%	Needed for growth, repair and general development.
Fat	Approx. 10–40%	Needed for body heat and energy storage; amount dependent on housing and exercise regimes.
Fibre	Up to 4%	Needed for digestive aid. Ferrets cannot tolerate levels in excess of 4%.

The basic nutritional requirements of ferrets.

The above are rough figures only and really only apply to dry foods. Naturally, other vitamins and minerals are also required, but in little more than trace element quantities. If feeding on dry food, copious amounts of water must be supplied. Ferrets fed on an entirely dry diet can, and often do, consume up to three times the volume of water to food. Should the water supply be allowed to run dry, they will often stop eating.

The above having been taken into account, it must always be remembered that ferrets are carnivores, meat eaters. In the wild, their natural diet would be one of meat. They would hunt down their prey, kill and eat it.

Their 'taste' is broad and varied; it would include basically any form of flesh whether it be from mammals, birds, fish, reptiles, worms, even slugs and snails, and they would also not be above robbing nests. They catch and kill their meal, then proceed to eat it – the whole carcass. Just because they are now living in captivity with us, why should we consider their diet to be different? How on earth can anyone justify keeping an animal whose natural diet is as above on rubbish such as milk sops! (A mixture of bread and milk.) It is no wonder that in the past captive ferrets led very short lives in comparison with the expected norm.

Logically, the best diet for us to give them would be one of cadavers, provided that they are fresh, although I would recommend first removing the stomach and intestines. (After all, they are little more than thin skin and rubbish that will probably end up as a mess in the court or cage.)

The liver should be inspected for signs of disease and discarded if any is found. The fur or feathers should be left on as this provides fibre in their diet, but be aware of the fact that you may be introducing ticks or fleas.

Should any form of fresh food be given – by fresh I mean other than dry food – all remnants must be removed from the ferrets' environment the day after its introduction. Under no circumstances should it be left until it has all gone, as food poisoning will possibly result. A consideration that has to be remembered here is that ferrets are natural hoarders, so you will have to search their domicile thoroughly for all traces of the food and be sure to remove it all.

It is highly unlikely that you will have access to a good enough supply of fresh cadavers to feed your ferrets on a regular basis. Dry food is a good alternative, and there are several varieties available to choose from that are currently on the market. However, the options do not stop here, as there are other alternatives too.

CAT AND DOG FOOD

There are a number of commercially produced canned cat and dog foods on the market. They are obviously not formulated for ferrets but are an acceptable alternative. Cat food, generally speaking, tends to have a higher protein value and by virtue of this fact is the better of the two options.

However, no matter which option you choose I would be inclined to add a vitamin supplement such as Intervet SA-37. I believe it is available in two packaging alternatives, 200g tubs and 2kg tubs. It is usually available from good pet shops or veterinary surgeries; alternatively, ask your vet for his/her recommendation.

Amongst the various dried cat and dog foods available, I have found a particular dried cat food to be ideal. The nutritional breakdown of it is virtually identical to that of commercially produced dried ferret food, it is a fraction of the price, and my ferrets love it and are in great condition.

Distinct advantages of dried food options are that the ferrets' faeces tend to be firmer, and smell less strongly – although this should not be a concern if you clean them on a daily basis, as should be the case. A further advantage and one of much greater importance is that as long as it remains dry, it will not 'go off'.

DAY-OLD CHICKS

Many people thought this to be a good source of food. It is relatively inexpensive and fairly freely available. However, it is not a food to be recommended for frequent use.

Research has discovered that day-old chicks are low in some essential requirements, leading to serious health problems in ferrets such as osteodystrophy, hypocalcaemia and thiamine deficiency, to name but a few. Another complaint caused by excessive feeding of these to ferrets in particular is actinomycosis.

Actinomycosis is a condition that causes the throat to thicken and swell. It is thought to be the result of abrasions within the oesophagus, precipitated by feeding too many day-old chicks. My ferrets are given chicks occasionally; generally speaking they are never fed on chicks more than once or twice per month.

Another food option, and one which I use frequently, is to prepare the meals myself. I have a reasonable supply of trimmings from a fast-food outlet, purchase offal from a butcher, and then cut it all up and cook it. Once cooked and cool, I mince it. It can then be packed into conveniently sized portions and frozen for use as required. Before feeding, it must be thoroughly thawed out, and I do mean thoroughly, a food additive such as Intervet SA-37 is sprinkled onto it, and then it is fed to the ferrets.

Because the mixture has been cooked, I find that it does not carry the risk of going off as quickly as raw meat, nor does it attract as many flies, and because it is minced the ferrets cannot carry it off and hoard it very easily, thereby making my husbandry tasks much less complicated.

Whatever your chosen food option may be, things to be guarded against are too much liver, as the vitamins contained within it can be harmful if fed in too great a quantity, and too many raw eggs for the same reason.

A further consideration, curious as it may sound, is to avoid feeding too much 'good meat'. Ferrets must always be given good, fresh meat, but in addition to the muscle or lean tissue, they must also be given some fat, and it is good for them also to have items such as the 'lights' or lungs of animals mixed in with the good meat.

In addition to food, clean water must obviously always be available. Should the water supply run out for any reason, ferrets will often stop eating. In the interests of hygiene, it is best to supply water via pet drinking bottles, but they must be refreshed on a daily basis.

Drinking dishes should be avoided, because the cage litter can get into them, thereby polluting them. The ferrets can walk in them, again polluting them, and they are easily spilt. Should they be spilt, not only do the ferrets go short of water, but the housing environment becomes wet and unpleasant, not to mention the risk of causing foot rot. Another reason for their avoidance is that should you be breeding, kittens could get into a dish of water and drown.

The above points having been taken into consideration, when using the drinker bottles, particularly if you reside in a hard-water area, the inside of the metal spout must be checked frequently for the accumulation of limescale, as this can build up quite quickly and occlude the pipe, thereby cutting off the water supply from the bottle.

7

Housing and Handling

HOUSING

The first point to be considered with reference to ferret housing is that it must be secure. If a mustelid finds a hole that it can get its head through, then it will generally be capable of getting the rest of its body through and escaping. Therefore all housing needs to be strong and secure to begin with. It must also be checked for damage and weaknesses regularly and any remedial action taken promptly should the need arise.

Cages can be bought from good pet shops, or can be relatively easily constructed by oneself. If ferrets are kept outside, then another option for their housing other than independent cages would be to build courts for them in order that they can be housed communally.

Keeping ferrets communally is always a far better and preferential option to keeping them singly in my opinion. They are gregarious creatures, in captivity, and benefit greatly from each other's company. They will be more at ease and far happier with the company of others, they will play happily together, and they will also extend their own cleaning and hygiene activities to their companions, washing and grooming each other.

The minimum suitable size of unit to house two ferrets would be one of approximately 5ft (1.5m) long, 19.5in (500mm) high and 23.5in (600mm) deep. The bed should be approximately 12in (300mm) wide with a hole approximately 4in (100mm) in diameter connecting it to the run. It should also have holes at the top of the door to afford ventilation in order that the occupants do not overheat. As with the aforementioned breeding unit, the wire on the door should be twill-weld or weldmesh with holes no greater than 0.5in (13mm) square.

If it is to be kept outside, the cage should be situated somewhere cool, in the shade if possible, and away from draughts. It should never be sited in a position where it will be subjected to direct sunlight, because it will become hot and the occupants will then suffer from heatstroke. Ferrets, like many small animals, have difficulty controlling their body temperature. In the case of ferrets this situation is further exacerbated because they are unable to sweat due to the fact that they have no sweat glands.

If the second housing option of courts is chosen, size is limited only by the available space and budget. If you are planning to keep multiple ferrets, courts are, in my opinion, a far better housing environment because the ferrets then have more room to exercise. Various items can also be provided for them to climb and play both in and on without cramping their environment. Again, as with cages, the courts should be constructed preferably in the shade and away from draughts. Direct sunlight should again be avoided at all costs.

Whichever housing option is used, all timber should be treated with a good-quality water repellent and preservative when they are completed. Ideally, water-based treatments should be used for this purpose, as they tend to be more animal-friendly.

Roofs should also be waterproofed with materials such as good-quality mineral roofing felt in the case of cages, and suitable roofing materials should be used in the case of courts. The ferret's environment should always be kept clean and dry to avoid ailments such as foot rot. Lavatory corners or areas should be scraped or otherwise cleaned on a daily basis.

PICKING UP

The handling of young kittens has been covered in the section on breeding. The handling of adults is naturally somewhat different. Before the question of methods of holding can be addressed, however, one first has to pick up the ferret.

It should always be remembered that when approaching a ferret you must never lunge towards them, particularly from above. Should this be done the ferret will almost certainly perceive the approach as an attack from a predator. It will naturally react defensively, probably biting. It will also result in the ferret becoming skulky and difficult to pick up or handle.

Ideally, if a hand is offered out, flat on the ground, palm uppermost, then the ferret will walk onto it. Once the ferret has stepped onto the outstretched hand and has walked up as far as having its hands on the open palm, then the index finger and second finger can be curled upward, one on either side of the chest, behind the arms. From here, the ferret can easily be picked up, but as soon as possible the other hand must be placed under the hindquarters to support the body weight.

Alternatively, the ferret can be grasped gently, index finger and thumb around the neck, with the other three fingers around the chest. This type of grip must only be used gently, because if the grip is too tight it not surprisingly becomes known as 'strangling'.

In this situation, the ferret is likely to perceive the situation to be threatening, and struggle to get free, possibly biting. The situation will then probably evolve into a vicious circle, with the ferret struggling more and the handler gripping more tightly. The ferret will at some point almost certainly bite; both handler and ferret will be hurt – an ugly situation that can be so easily avoided with careful handling.

HOLDING

Once a ferret has been picked up, there are basically two correct methods of holding it. The first method is the same as the second method of picking up that is detailed above, with the index finger and thumb of one hand around the neck and the remaining three fingers around the chest, this being supplemented with the other hand under the hindquarters supporting the body weight. This is my preferred method of holding, as I feel it is the most gentle.

The second method of holding a ferret is to grasp and hold it by the scruff of the neck in one hand, in a similar manner to that which is used to pick up a cat. This method is again supplemented by supporting the body weight with the other hand.

Whilst this method is acceptable, I consider it to be somewhat more brutal than the first method, although it is very useful at times because it tends to render the ferret more docile. If this method is employed, the ferret will often hang motionless. This is of greatest value should you need to open the ferrret's mouth to inspect its dentition or oral health.

On occasions, ferrets will bite. This is not a pleasant situation, and certainly not one that should be allowed to continue unaddressed. Just because a ferret has bitten in the past, and still bites, it does not necessarily mean that it is vicious and unhandleable. It can usually be retrained with care, compassion and proper handling.

Firstly, it must be dissuaded from biting. When it actually bites, it should be flicked firmly on the nose with the back of a fingernail. Another form of discipline that I have found to be extremely effective

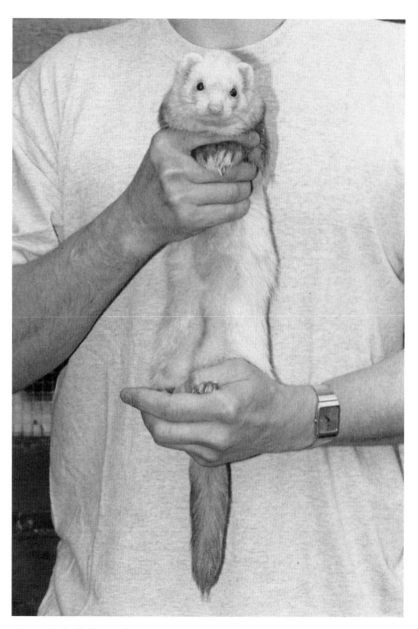

One method of holding a ferret.

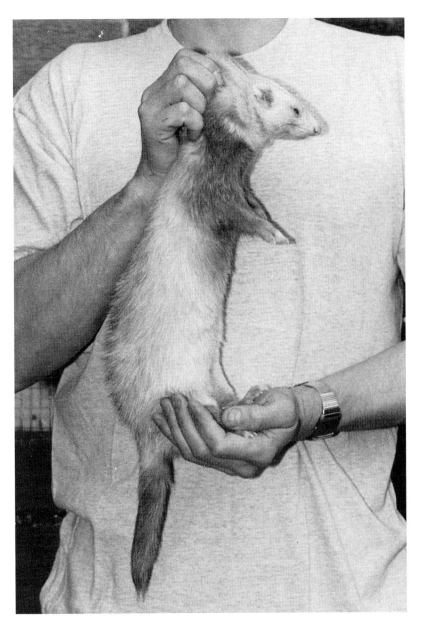

The second method of holding a ferret.

is to shake the animal by the scruff of the neck. I assume that this method works because it is the way that the dam would discipline her kittens.

The first of the two methods of discipline listed above relies on the relationship of unwanted behaviour being accompanied with the receipt of pain. The second, and my preferred option, reduces the situation psychologically to a level that the ferret has understood as discipline from an early age, as it was administered in this way by its mother.

As with all training of animals, far more and far better results are obtained with the use of kindness. Whilst the unwanted behaviour must be curtailed with discipline, good behaviour must also be propagated and rewarded with the giving of praise and treats or rewards. With diligence and care, over a period of time, the unwanted behaviour should be eradicated and a well-behaved ferret will be the result.

8

Colour Standards

The following colour standards and requirements are reproduced, with permission, from the website of the American Ferret Association, Inc.

BASIC COLOUR STANDARDS

Albino

The guard hairs must be white to cream, with white being preferable. The undercoat must also be white to cream, again with white being preferable. Eyes must be red only, and the nose must be pink.

Black

The guard hairs must be black, and the undercoat is preferably white, although a slight golden hue is acceptable. The eyes must be black or near black, and the nose must be black, although speckled black is acceptable.

Black Sable

The guard hairs must be dark ash blackish-brown, with no warm brown tone, and with a noticeable black glossy shine. The undercoat is preferred to be white to cream, but not yellow. Eyes must be dark brown or near to black, and the nose is preferred to be ash blackish-brown, although mottled or heavy speckled blackish-brown is acceptable.

Champagne

Guard hairs are to be tan or a diluted form of chocolate, and the undercoat is to be white to cream, but not yellow. Eyes are to be light to dark burgundy, and the nose is preferred to be beige, or it can be pink or pink with a beige or light brown 'T' outline.

Chocolate

Guard hairs are to be a warm milk-chocolate brown, and the under-coat is preferred to be white, but a slight golden hue is acceptable. Eyes are preferred to be brown, but a dark burgundy is acceptable. The nose is preferred to be pink, beige or pink with a light brown 'T' outline, although a brick nose colour is acceptable.

Cinnamon

The guard hairs are to be a rich light reddish-brown, and the under-coat is to be white to cream, with white being preferable. The eyes must be burgundy, the nose is preferred to be brick-coloured, beige or pink with a light brown or brick-coloured 'T' outline. Pink is allowed, but not preferred.

Sable

The guard hairs must be a warm deep brown, and the undercoat is preferred to be white to cream or light golden, but not yellow. The eyes must be brown or near black, and the nose is preferred to be a light brown, speckled or mottled brown, or with a brown 'T' outline.

COLOUR CONCENTRATION PATTERN STANDARDS

Point (Siamese)

The colour concentration will show a distinct difference in colour concentration between the body colour and the points. The mask must be a thin 'V' mask for black, black sable, sable, cinnamon, and chocolate, not a full 'T' bar mask. Champagnes may have a 'V' mask, or no mask. The nose colour should be lighter than the above stated nose colours, meaning pink, beige or 'T' outline.

Roans

The colour concentration will be 50 per cent to 60 per cent coloured guard hairs of any colour, with 40 per cent to 50 per cent white guard hairs. The mask and nose colours are dependent on the colour and underlying pattern.

Solids

The colour concentration should be such that the percentage of coloured guard hairs should ideally be 100 per cent in relation to white guard hairs, which should ideally be 0 per cent in the body and the points, giving the appearance of solid colour concentration from head to tail. The mask should be full or 'T' bar, and the nose should be appropriate for the colour standard.

Standards

The colour concentration should be that the percentage of coloured guard hairs should be approximately 90 per cent to 100 per cent in relation to white guard hairs, but the colour concentration is not as heavy as it is in the solid pattern. The body will appear lighter in colour concentration and the points will be easily discernible. The mask will be either full or 'T' bar, and the nose will be appropriate for the colour standard.

WHITE MARKING PATTERN STANDARDS

Blaze

The head markings must be such that there is a long white blaze from the forehead, between the ears and down the back of the neck, preferably to the shoulders. The mask will vary depending on the colour concentration standard. Minor colour rings around the eyes and small masks are acceptable, but full masks are not acceptable. The eyes should be of varying shades of ruby to brown, and the nose should be pink or pink with a light outline. The front and hind feet should have white tips or mitts. Other acceptable markings are knee patches and a white tip on the tail. Bib, white or speckled bellies and roaning are also acceptable.

Panda

The preferred panda should have an almost completely white head that includes the neck and throat. Coloured guard hairs forming eye rings are acceptable. The eyes should be varying shades of burgundy and the nose should be pink, or pink with a light outline. Mitts should be present on all four feet. Knee patches may be present and a white tip on the tail is also acceptable.

Mitts

Masks and other head markings should be appropriate for the colour concentration standard and eyes should be varying shades of burgundy. The nose colour is dependent on the body colour standard, and mitts should be present on all four feet. Bib and knee patches may be present and a white tip on the tail is acceptable.

Colour Pattern Combination Chart

	Albino	Black	Black Sable	Champagne	Chocolate	Cinnamon	DEW & DEW Pattern	Sable
Blaze	N/A	Black Blaze	Black Sable Blaze	Champagne Blaze	Chocolate Blaze	Cinnamon Blaze	N/A	Sable Blaze
Panda	N/A	Black Panda	Black Sable Panda	Champagne Panda	Chocolate Panda	Cinnamon Panda	N/A	Sable Panda
Point (Siamese)	N/A	Black Point	N/A	Champagne Point	Chocolate Point	Cinnamon Point	N/A	Sable Point
Roans	N/A	Black Roan (also known as medium silver)	Black Sable Roan	Champagne Roan	Chocolate Roan	Cinnamon Roan	N/A	Sable Roan
Solid	N/A	Black Solid (only applicable with mitts, known as a black mitt)	Black Sable Solid	Champagne Solid	Chocolate Solid	Cinnamon Solid	N/A	Sable Solid
Standard		Black Standard (only applicable with mitts, known as a black mitt)	Black Sable Standard	Champagne Standard	Chocolate Standard	Cinnamon Standard	N/A	Sable Standard

Notes:

Albino is the absence of pigment (guard hairs will be white) and the absence of pattern.

A noticeable colour difference exists between cinnamons and champagnes; cinnamons will display a strong reddish cast to the guard hairs. Cinnamons are not as common as champagnes.

Solids, standards, roans and points can also have white mitts (ie. sable standard mitt, sable roan mitt, sable point mitt, and so on.

DEW is the abbreviation for 'Dark-Eyed White'. All DEWs will be called 'dark-eyed white', or 'dark-eyed white patterns' regardless of which other colour is present.

9

Health and Welfare

Ferret illnesses and diseases is a very large subject on its own, and one that I believe to be beyond the scope of this book. Another factor to be considered is that even if we, as laypeople, could make an accurate diagnosis we still would not have access to the necessary drugs and medicines required to treat the ailing ferret. Therefore we would need to consult a veterinary surgeon in any case. That having been said, I consider it to be responsible behaviour for any animal keeper to learn as much as possible about the health and welfare of his or her charges. As previously stated, this is a large subject all of its own and consequently a number of books have been compiled or written about it. They are available to borrow from libraries, or if preferred they can be purchased at any number of outlets.

With the above borne in mind, it is essential in my opinion to examine your ferrets thoroughly on a daily basis. This can easily be done at feeding time, for example, and it does not take long.

If your ferrets are kept communally, or have recently been mated, particular attention should be given to the area around the neck and ears in case bites have penetrated the skin. Should any puncture wounds be found they should be bathed with warm salty water to cleanse them and hopefully prevent infection.

Watch how the ferrets move and thoroughly examine them. In the event of any cause for concern being discovered the ferret should be taken to a veterinary surgeon as soon as possible. Ferrets are extremely hardy creatures and rarely display signs of illness until the problem is well advanced. This obviously makes it more difficult to treat, thereby reducing the chances of a full recovery.

I would always advise anyone to consider very carefully which practitioner he or she chooses to consult with. These investigations can and should be made prior to the need for consultation arising, in order that when required you know exactly which vet to contact to get the best care possible for your ferret. Not all vets are conversant with ferrets; therefore you should make your selection very carefully. The best way to find vets that are well experienced in dealing with ferrets is to try to find out if there is a ferret club of any kind in your area – they will tell you which vet they use. If this option is not available, then you will have to use a more direct approach. Locate the veterinary practices in your area and either telephone or visit them. Ask if they have treated ferrets and, if so, how much experience they have relating to them.

With the above taken into consideration I will now proceed to list some of the more common complaints, along with their clinical presentation, in order that you will have some point of reference when examining your ferrets.

ABSCESSES

Abscesses generally begin as a wound that becomes infected and fills with pus. The most common site is usually in or around the neck. There are a number of possible causes, the most likely being: bites sustained during fights, play or mating; and damage to the inside of the mouth or throat by sharp objects such as bones in their food.

• Clinical presentation is a swelling or lump.

Treatment is usually by lancing or surgically removing the problem, identifying and rectifying the cause, and treating the animal with a course of broad-spectrum antibiotics.

ACTINOMYCOSIS

This is a hardening and swelling of the ferret's oesophagus. It is thought to be precipitated by the feeding of too many day-old chicks, causing abrasions within the oesophagus.

• Clinical presentation is a swollen and hard neck, anorexia, listlessness and fever.

The veterinary surgeon will treat the animal by giving injections, and you will need to feed it on a liquid diet until it is recovered.

ALEUTIAN DISEASE

Although not particularly common, this disease is contagious and fatal. It gets its name from the Aleutian strain of mink, due to the fact that it was first discovered in them in America during the 1950s. It is an immune-deficiency disease, caused by a parvovirus. It can be passed genetically from parents to offspring, or between ferrets in bodily fluids. These need not be from any physical contact; simply an infected ferret coughing or sneezing can pass it. The aerosol droplets resulting from this action can transmit the disease to others up to a metre away.

• Clinical presentations include: weight loss; lethargy; rear leg weakness; anorexia; tarry faeces; intermittent head tremor; diarrhoea; faecal and urinary incontinence; aggressiveness; and fevers. Ultimately, unless the animal is the subject of euthanasia, it will die.

There is no specific treatment, no cure and no vaccine.

ALOPECIA

This is hair loss. It may be localized, or over the entire animal. It can occur in any gender, at any age, and for a number of reasons. These include: the feeding of too many raw eggs; mites; nervous reaction; or just excessive moult.

• Clinical presentation obviously is lack of hair.

Consulting a vet is essential; he or she will examine the ferret, take skin scrapings if necessary for analysis, and treat the animal accordingly. Often hair will grow back at next moult.

BITES AND STINGS

Ferrets potentially can suffer bites from a number of sources: from other ferrets during play or more likely in the breeding season; or from snakes, rats or other predators whilst out working. Other possibilities are from insect bites or stings.

• Clinical presentation is a lump or perforation of the ferret's skin.

A small amount of hair or fur should be clipped from the immediate vicinity of the wound. Careful examination should be made to ensure that there is no foreign body or material present in the wound; if anything is discovered it must be removed carefully with tweezers. The wound should then be bathed with a strong saline solution and treated with antiseptic.

Note: If the wound is around the throat, it may be necessary to seek veterinary advice. Should the site swell, it might cause occlusion of the airways, thereby risking the ferret's life.

BOTULISM

Botulism is probably one of the most prevalent killers of ferrets, and is so easily preventable. It is caused by a bacterium, namely *Clostridium botulinum*. In the event of this bacteria coming into contact with decaying flesh, a deadly toxin results. Should this 'food' then be ingested, botulism is contracted. It attacks the ferret's nervous system.

• Clinical presentation is usually paralysis, commonly originating in the hindquarters and spreading to the vital organs, causing death.

There is no cure for this disease. Prevention is the only defence; this is why great care must be taken to ensure that any remnants of uneaten food are removed from the ferret's environment.

BROKEN TEETH

Ferrets can fairly easily break their teeth whilst out working. It can also be a result of biting or chewing things within their environment.

• Clinical presentation is easily visible; however, your attention may be first attracted by the ferret apparently exhibiting difficulty in eating normally, that is, chewing on one side or displaying discomfort during eating. In severe cases, which should never occur as the problem should be identified early during regular examinations, weight loss will be apparent.

Veterinary attention must be sought.

CANCER

This is an illness that ferrets can be prone to suffer from. It is potentially fatal. It is not contagious and, if diagnosed early enough, can be surgically treated.

• Clinical presentations are usually lumps or swellings on the body of the ferret, or solid masses can be detected internally by palpation. In the case of gastric carcinoma, in its advanced stages, the ferret will become lethargic and weak, appetite will be lost, and on occasions when food is taken, it will be vomited back shortly afterward. I particularly mention gastric carcinoma because I am led to believe that it is not uncommon in ferrets.

If suspected, veterinary attention must be sought at the earliest possible time, and advice taken. In advanced cases, euthanasia will probably be recommended in the interests of kindness.

CANINE DISTEMPER

This is a virus that ferrets are particularly prone to contract. It is fatal. The incubation period is seven to nine days, and dogs are the most likely source of infection. It is a highly contagious disease, and as soon as it is suspected the affected animals must be isolated or quarantined. It is only treatable in its early stages, and it is often better to terminate the affected animals once the diagnosis is confirmed.

• Clinical presentations are: a rash on the chin; the skin surrounding the lips and chin swells and becomes crusty, often accompanied by dermatitis on the anus; photophobia; anorexia; depression; swollen feet, followed by the pads hardening; runny eyes and nose; reduction in appetite; increased thirst; and diarrhoea. If the animal is not the subject of euthanasia, it may well vomit, suffer convulsions and become comatose prior to death.

CANKER

The same mite that causes the infection in cats and dogs causes canker of the ears in ferrets. Generally, ferrets contract it from them, and a common cause of the cross-infection is ferrets and dogs travelling in close proximity to one another in a car, on the way to a day's rabbiting.

- Clinical presentations are the ferret becoming drowsy, possibly lethargic, and reduction in and sometimes loss of appetite. These symptoms are accompanied by a discharge of wax from the ear(s).

Veterinary consultation is imperative, particularly in the case of young ferrets, as it can lead to meningitis, with fatal consequences in their case.

CATARACTS

A jill ferret with cataracts; most visible in her left eye, as the cloudy or opaque region.

This is a condition that I have seen very frequently in ferrets. The affected animal feels no pain, and manages remarkably well considering that it has lost its sight. This is partly due, I believe, to the fact that a ferret's eyesight is not particularly good anyway, and partly because in the working environment, it operates in subterranean tunnels where it could not see even if it were to have perfect sight!

Ferrets normally rely mainly on their ears, nose and whiskers for the gathering of sensory information.

• Clinical presentation is of a ferret whose eyes, on examination, appear opaque or cloudy.

I do not know of any surgical treatments being available, and, as long as the ferret is comfortable and manages to live with quality of life, let it continue to do so.

EAR MITES

These are a pest, and, as the name suggests, they infest the ears. They are unfortunately common in ferrets, and should they migrate down the aural canal they could cause the middle ear to become infected. They are not visible to the naked eye, therefore an otoscope is required to see them.

• Clinical presentation is: head shaking; ear scratching; walking with the head tilted to one side; staggers or balance problems; and an exudate of thick brown wax.

A vet must be consulted, and the animal will be treated with a course of injections or eardrops. All animals that have been in contact with the affected one must also be treated. All bedding materials and cage litter must be removed and burnt and replaced with fresh, or the problem will recur. Under no circumstances should an untrained person attempt to clean anything but the outermost parts of the ears as damage can easily be done.

FLEAS

These are parasites that, if allowed, will inhabit the coat of the ferret, making its life a misery.

• Clinical presentation is usually excessive scratching, hair loss and possibly blood spots in the coat.

Treatment is the same as for cats. I would recommend getting a product such as Frontline Spray from your veterinary surgeon, spraying a

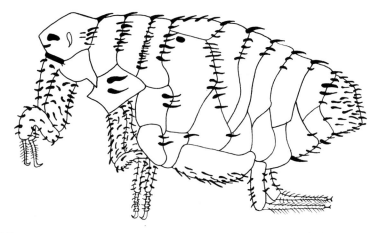

A flea.

small amount onto a rubber glove and stroking it into the ferret's coat thoroughly. All animals that come into contact with the affected individual must also be treated, and the bedding and domicile litter burnt and replaced with fresh to prevent recurrence of the problem. The cage or court should be treated with a suitable pesticide.

(*Note*: Pregnant or nursing jills in particular should not be treated due to the risk of harming or killing the offspring. Seek veterinary advice.)

GASTROINTESTINAL FOREIGN BODIES

These, as the name implies, are abnormal objects inside the animal's intestines, causing a blockage. In young ferrets they are probably most likely to be pieces of sponge or rubber torn or chewed from their toys; it is for this reason that any toys or items supplied for the amusement of ferrets must be selected very carefully. In older ferrets the obstruction is more likely to be caused by trichobezoars (hair balls) that have accumulated, most often during the ferret's moulting period.

- Clinical presentations are: lethargy; reduced appetite; anorexia; diarrhoea; vomiting; nausea; and weakness. Sometimes the obstruction can be palpated by gently examining the animal's abdomen. Alternatively, and quite often a necessity for confirmation, X-rays will need to be taken.

Occasionally, small obstructions can be induced to pass naturally with the use of intestinal lubricants such as cat laxatives. More commonly, surgical removal is required. Recovery is generally quite rapid. As ever, prevention is far better than cure. Toys and other items that the ferrets are allowed access to should be considered carefully, and cat laxatives can be employed during moulting.

GINGIVITIS

This is a gum disorder, which may lead to loss of teeth or further infections.

• Clinical presentation is of 'angry', inflamed gums and bad breath. The ferret exhibiting difficulty in eating, as previously described in relation to broken teeth, may attract your attention.

Veterinary advice must be sought.

HEATSTROKE

This condition is commonly referred to as 'the sweats', quite erroneously due to the fact that ferrets are incapable of sweating as they have no sweat glands! It is most commonly caused by lack of thought when positioning the cage, that is, not allowing or creating enough shade. Another cause is lack of thought when out working, such as leaving the carrying box in direct sunlight or even in a locked vehicle, where temperatures can rise dramatically.

• Clinical presentation is usually an agitated ferret, often in distress. If the situation arises in their cage, the ferrets will often stretch out in an attempt to cool themselves, and pant heavily. If no action is taken, or action is not taken promptly enough, then they will pass out, become comatose, and eventually die.

At the first suspicion of heatstroke, act immediately. The animal is overheating; therefore you must cool both it and its environment down. In extremely mild cases you may simply be able to reposition the cage in a more suitable place, something that has to be done in any case. Usually, the situation will be more severe and you will have to take more drastic measures. By far the best way of cooling the ferret down, without shocking it, is to spray it with cool water. Also encourage it to drink cool water, from a dish if necessary. If after these emergency steps have been taken you have any further concerns, consult a vet.

HYPOCALCAEMIA

This is a lack of calcium in the blood, usually caused by the feeding of an inadequate diet. It is usually discovered whilst investigating the cause of conditions such as posterior paralysis through routine blood analysis.

Treatment is commonly via injections and feeding calcium-rich diets.

INFLUENZA

A number of strains of the human influenza virus can infect ferrets. Transmission of the disease from humans to ferrets, ferrets to humans, and ferret to ferret is easily accomplished in aerosol droplets carried on the breath.

- Clinical presentations are: coughing; sneezing; runny eyes and nose; lethargy; and sometimes photophobia and conjunctivitis occur. Very young kits may develop a much more severe upper respiratory infection, leading to death after a lower airway obstruction.

A veterinary surgeon should be consulted with reference to treatment; also it is good to offer favourite foods to keep the ferret's strength up and actively to encourage plenty of drinking to prevent dehydration.

LICE

This is another parasite that is sometimes, though not often, found on ferrets. It is an external pest, and if you work your ferrets they will be

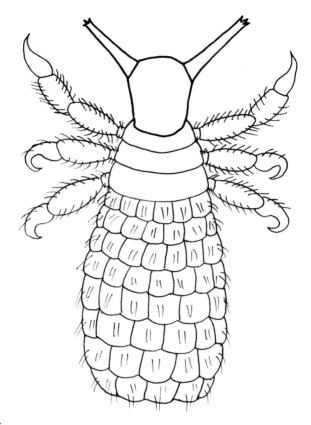

A louse.

almost certain to come into contact with them at some point in their lives.

- Clinical presentation is similar to fleas, in that the ferret will be scratching excessively, and there may be blood spots in the coat as a result of this.

It is easily dealt with by applying a treatment of good-quality pesticide, such as Frontline Spray. As with fleas and ticks, all bedding and so on must be burnt and replaced, and the cage or court treated.

(*Note*: Again, as with ticks and fleas, pregnant or nursing jills in particular should not be treated due to the risk of harming or killing the kits.)

MASTITIS

This is the inflammation of a jill's mammary glands. It usually occurs shortly after the birth of a litter, or after the third week of lactation when the kittens tend to demand large quantities of milk. This stresses the mother, and, in addition to this, the kits have teeth that can damage the nipples. It is a very painful condition that requires immediate medical attention.

- Clinical presentations are that the nipples are firm, usually red or purple in colour, hard and painful to the jill. The kits will probably be able to obtain little or even no milk. In acute cases the glands may become gangrenous in as little as hours after first being noticed. If this happens, the tissue turns black, and the jill will become extremely ill and dehydrated.

The ferret must be treated by a veterinary surgeon immediately. She will be treated with broad-spectrum antibiotics. In the case of gangrenous nipples, the necrotic tissue will have to be surgically removed. The handler must wash his or her hands thoroughly after handling the ill ferret before handling others to prevent the infection spreading.

OESTROGEN-INDUCED ANAEMIA

When a jill is in oestrus (season) the levels of oestrogen in her body rise significantly. If she is not brought out of season her health will be seriously affected. She will become anaemic, due to the depression of her bone marrow, which in severe cases can result in a condition called pancytopenia.

- Clinical presentations are: anaemia (characterized by pale lips and gums); loss of weight; anorexia; alopecia; respiratory problems; darkening of faeces; and sores.

Feeding her on raw red meat may be beneficial in mild cases, but in more serious cases blood transfusions will be required and may still not be effective. Prevention is far better than cure and this situation can be easily avoided. To get her out of oestrus there are three options: she can be mated with a hob; she can be served by a hoblet (vasectomized hob); or she can be taken to a veterinary surgeon who will administer a 'jill jab'(an injection of hormones to bring her out of oestrus). The alternative to these, but which is obviously only possible if you never want to breed from her, is to have her spayed.

PANCYTOPENIA

This condition is the abnormal depression of all three elements of a ferret's blood. Usually it develops pursuant to the previously mentioned oestrogen-induced anaemia. It is seriously debilitating and likely to prove fatal.

• Clinical presentation is as for oestrogen-induced anaemia: muscular wasting; loss of weight; anorexia; alopecia; paleness of lips and gums; and respiratory difficulties.

Blood tests will need to be made for confirmation. Blood transfusions may be beneficial; however, treatment is not likely to be effective. Euthanasia is probably the kindest route.

POSTERIOR PARALYSIS

This condition is also often referred to as 'the staggers'. There are multiple possible causes of paralysis in ferrets – they may be neurological, physical, or even dietary. Some potential causes include: Aleutian disease; hypocalcaemia; spinal carcinoma; viral myelitis; vertebral trauma precipitated by injury; or the feeding of an inadequate diet.

• Clinical presentations are: muscular wasting in the hindquarters; weakness; inability to move in a normal manner; lethargy; loss of sensation in the extremities; and loss of voluntary movement.

Veterinary consultation should be sought immediately.

PYOMETRA

This is a condition where pus accumulates within the uterus of a jill. It can occur after the start of a pseudo-pregnancy (phantom pregnancy, the result of being served by a hoblet), or on occasion when a jill is left in oestrus too long.

- Clinical presentations are typically: anorexia; lethargy; dehydration; and fever. The vulva will be swollen and there may also be a discharge.

Medical attention must be sought urgently. In some cases the patient will respond well to a course of antibiotics; ensuring that she drinks plenty of water to prevent or combat dehydration is also very important. In more serious cases, an ovariohysterectomy will have to be performed, sometimes immediately, in order that the uterus is prevented from rupturing, which would precipitate peritonitis.

RENAL FAILURE

This is the dysfunction, or failure to operate, of the ferret's kidneys. The condition can be, in some cases, a transitory event and in such instances the animal will recover. However, it is more commonly terminal.

- Clinical presentations are: a loss in general condition; severe weight loss; reduction in, or loss of, appetite for food; increased drinking; and foul-smelling breath. On palpation, the kidneys can feel hard.

Medical attention should be sought. The foul breath and appetite problems alone could, for example, be caused by a relatively simple oral problem such as gingivitis, not this more sinister possibility. If renal failure is suspected, blood tests can be performed for the purpose of confirmation of the diagnosis. Should this be so, euthanasia is recommended in the interests of kindness as there is no cure and the animal would otherwise waste away and die slowly, without dignity.

TICKS

These are parasites that infest the ferret; they bite through the skin and suck blood from the host animal. Some would suggest the burning of the tick with a lighted cigarette. I cannot agree with this, as it is far too easy to burn the ferret instead. There are various tools on the market for the removal of such pests. However, whichever method is employed be sure to remove all of the tick. It is far too easy to leave the mouthparts behind and this will potentially result in an abscess.

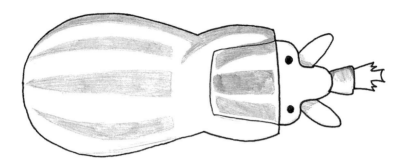

A tick.

I have heard it said that if you grasp the tick between your finger and thumb and rotate it one and a half times, it will let go and be easily removed. I cannot say whether this is true or not, as I have never tried it.

- Clinical presentation is of an external parasite attached to the ferret's body.

On occasions when I have had to deal with these pests I use a pair of thin, curved tweezers to grasp the tick by its mouthparts and remove it. Again, I feel that prevention is better than cure and I treat the ferrets' coats periodically as previously described with Frontline Spray. As with all parasitic infestations, all bedding and litter must be removed and burnt and the domicile treated prior to installing fresh litter and bedding. (*Note:* pregnant or nursing jills in particular should not be treated due to the risk of harming or killing the young.)

TRICHOBEZOARS

These are balls of hair that accumulate within the intestines of the affected animal. The most common time for this occurrence is during a period of moulting. They can cause the normal passage of food to be inhibited, resulting in illness and possibly death.

- Clinical presentations are: loss of appetite; lethargy; listlessness; visible pain and discomfort; vomiting; and weight loss. Sometimes experienced or trained hands may be able to identify the mass by gentle palpation.

Veterinary attention must be sought. Sometimes small masses can be induced to be passed naturally with the employment of gastric lubricants, such as cat laxatives. More severe cases will warrant further investigation, usually by X-ray initially, followed by surgical removal. Recovery is commonly swift and the prognosis is good.

ZINC TOXICITY

This is a condition that should be relatively easy to prevent. Unfortunately, ferrets are unable to endure increased or high levels of zinc in their system. Primary sources of this metal in the ferrets' environment are items such as drinkers, feed dishes or other receptacles that are made of metal, which, in an attempt to increase their longevity, have been galvanized. Items such as these should, for preference, be manufactured from stainless steel, which eliminates them as a source of zinc. However, one other common utilization of this plating process is on the cage wires, which are typically galvanized twillweld or weldmesh. The ferrets generally ingest the zinc by licking or chewing at treated surfaces.

• Clinical presentations are: a weakness in the hindquarters; lethargy; and anaemia. Renal failure usually follows.

As in all cases of illness, a veterinary surgeon must be consulted for tests and diagnosis. If this condition is confirmed, there is no cure or treatment. Euthanasia will probably be recommended in the interests of kindness.

Index